THE COMPLETE BARBECUE COOKBOOK

THE COMPLETE BARBECUE COOKBOOK

EXPERT ADVICE AND FOOLPROOF RECIPES
FOR BBQ PERFECTION

STERLING SMITH

PHOTOGRAPHY BY DARREN MUIR

ROCKRIDGE
PRESS

Interior and Cover Designer: Scott A Wooledge
Art Producer: Janice Ackerman
Editor: Gurvinder Singh Gandu
Production Editor: Sigi Nacson
Production Manager: Jose Olivera

Photography: © Darren Muir; food styled by Yolanda Muir
Illustration: © Dima Kolchan, RU/The Noun Project
Author photo courtesy of Chris Loomis

Hardcover ISBN: 978-1-63878-6-085
Paperback ISBN: 978-1-63807-303-1
eBook ISBN: 978-1-63807-179-2
R0

Thank you to my amazing
wife and children, who
do nothing but love me
and support my barbecue
adventures. All of this is
possible because you lift me
up and make me a better
person every day.

Love Always,
Smitty (Dad)

CONTENTS

Introduction IX

INTRODUCTION

As a professional pitmaster who has traveled the world competing in over 100 events and teaching more than 80 barbecue cooking classes over the past several years, I have found that there is no replacement for education and knowledge. The more I have learned from my experiences lighting a fire, the classes I have attended, the books I have read, and my peers, the better cook I have become. When I first decided to get into barbecue, I ran out and bought a cheap smoker at a local hardware store and a bag of charcoal, some fresh mesquite wood chunks, and lighter fluid. On the way home I stopped at the neighborhood grocery store and picked up a huge bone-in pork shoulder and a bottle of random barbecue seasoning that was on sale. I got home, assembled the grill, and filled it with charcoal and about half a mesquite tree. I then doused it with a heavy dose of lighter fluid, lit the fire, and stood back. I had that grill smoking more than a freight train. Billowy whitish-gray smoke was leaking out of every hole in that smoker, and I thought I was barbecuing. I was amazed the local fire department didn't show up and shut me down. It was the absolute worst piece of meat I have ever tasted. The pork shoulder had black soot all over the surface, and it was drier than the desert. I did not know how to properly pick out a good piece of meat, how to set up and manage the fire in my grill, when or how to season properly, and, most important, I didn't know where to start.

At that point I knew I had a lot to learn. I wanted to get better and make tastier, juicier barbecue that my family and friends would rave about. I was on a mission. That was about 15 years ago, and since then I have won more than 750 barbecue awards and accolades, and I continue to travel the world teaching and spreading barbecue knowledge and love.

In this book I am going to share all the lessons and techniques I have learned along the way. You'll learn how to use your gas grill to "smoke," the hot-and-fast process versus low-and-slow cooking, how to achieve the most tasty, flavorful end results, and techniques for knowing when your food is done and how to rest your food properly. I am going to share some of my recipes and adaptations of recipes I have picked up during my barbecue adventures. I also provide some award-winning recipes from several of my best barbecue friends and colleagues.

Chapter 1

BARBECUE BASICS AND BEYOND

The word *barbecue* has many different definitions. It can mean the act of cooking food over fire, or it can mean a piece of equipment in which to cook food. It can be used to describe the flavor or taste of food cooked on a grill or pit, or to describe an event or social gathering in which barbecue food is served. Traditionally barbecue means low-and-slow cooking using wood as a fuel source. Beef brisket, pulled pork shoulder, chicken quarters, sausage, and turkey are traditional barbecue favorites served across the country. For our purposes, we will use the act of cooking meat over fire to define *barbecue*. This can be done low and slow with the fire cooking the food indirectly, or hot and fast, grilling the food directly over the coals or fire. I will include recipes and techniques for both styles of cooking in this book.

◀ Herb-Crusted Porchetta (page 82)

EQUIPPING YOUR BARBECUE KITCHEN

There are many different types of grills and smokers available on the market, from pellet grills to offset propane tank smokers and even homebuilt 55-gallon drum pits. We aren't going to get into each specific kind of grill and smoker available, and I am assuming most have a charcoal grill and/or a traditional gas grill. I recommend adding a smoker to your backyard barbecue kitchen if you do not have one. In addition to a smoker, there are several items that will make your barbecue experiences easier, tastier, and safer.

MEAT THERMOMETER

Having a good-quality meat thermometer is paramount in making sure your food reaches an internal temperature that is safe for consumption. Parasites and bacteria can live in meat proteins, and if not heated to certain levels, they can leave you and your guests very sick. I prefer the instant-read thermometers from ThermoWorks. They are sturdy, have a digital display, and give you a reading within seconds. Some lesser-quality thermometers may take up to a couple of minutes to get a reading. I use the end of the thermometer as a "probe" when testing for tenderness in large cuts like brisket, pork shoulder, and ribs.

GRILL GLOVES/HOT GLOVES

When I cook, I like to use my hands a lot. With that being said, I often burn myself, but I have found that using cotton knit gloves under a pair of nitrile latex gloves helps. They allows me to get a good feel of the meat while being able to withstand high heat. The gloves also help when I spin the grates on my grills or the food itself for even cooking and when I dump hot coals from a chimney lighter.

CHIMNEY LIGHTER

Using a chimney fire starter allows you to start your grill quicker, saving you time. It can be filled with charcoal briquettes or lump charcoal. I like to use two paraffin-wax fire starters under the chimney to get the fire going an hour or so before any food goes on the grill.

DISPOSABLE ALUMINUM FOIL PANS

I use these pans for multiple applications while cooking. You can put a pan opposite the fire to create a hot side and a cool side and to catch rendered fat drippings for easy cleanup; you can add water to the pan to create a moist cooking environment and regulate the grill temperature; or you can use foil pans to braise and create a steam bath in multiple recipes.

HEAVY-DUTY ALUMINUM FOIL

When purchasing aluminum foil, make sure to get heavy-duty. The foil is used to cover disposable aluminum pans to create a braise or to steam, to wrap meats at certain points throughout the cooking process to retain moisture or color, and to cover meats during resting.

TONGS AND SPATULAS

Handling hot food on the grill will be much easier with a good pair of spring-loaded tongs and a metal spatula. Tongs can also be used to mix items in a disposable aluminum pan and move hot coals or wood chunks around the fire.

DIRECT VS. INDIRECT COOKING

Basically, this is the difference between hot-and-fast grilling and low-and-slow barbecuing. In the first scenario, your food cooks directly over the hot coals, whereas in the second, the food cooks offset from the coals or the fire. Some proteins taste better cooked at a hot sear to seal in juices, but others benefit from a low-and-slow cook while a bark (or crust) forms and the fat renders at a slower rate. We will use both techniques for recipes in this book, as each produces delicious results.

DIRECT FIRE

To set up your grill for direct cooking, you will fill the entire charcoal basket or charcoal grate with lit coals from a charcoal chimney. You are looking for the entire surface of the grill to have an even amount of charcoal for consistent temperatures. If you are using a gas grill, you will light your grill as recommended by the manufacturer. If you have more than one burner, set all of them at an even temperature. This can range from high to low, and you will need to verify the analog or digital thermometer on most grill lids to get an idea of the internal temperature of the grill.

INDIRECT FIRE

For an indirect cooking setup, you will fill half the charcoal basket or grate with lit charcoal from a chimney lighter and place a disposable aluminum pan on the other side to create a two-zone cooking area. The pan can be used as a heat deflector, to catch rendered fat and drippings, and, when water is added, it will also create a moist cooking environment. Alternatively, the pan can be placed in the middle of the charcoal grate with the coals on each side. For a gas grill, you will light your grill as recommended by the manufacturer. If you have more than one burner, set half the burners to an even temperature, leaving the other burner(s) off (for two burners, have one on and one off; for a three-burner grill, have two off and one on). You will need to adjust the burner higher or lower based on the grill's internal temperature until it reaches your desired cooking temperature.

LIGHT MY FIRE

One of the most important steps in cooking is setting up your equipment properly and getting a good clean fire going. If you remember my first barbecue story, I had billowy whitish-gray smoke coming out of my smoker—that is not a clean fire. You are looking for smoke that is a light blue color or barely visible.

FOR A CHARCOAL GRILL

Place a chimney lighter on the charcoal basket area of your grill and fill it with charcoal briquettes or lump charcoal. Place two paraffin-wax lighter cubes under the chimney and light them with a long-handled lighter. After about 10 minutes, the cubes will burn out and the chimney will be lit. In roughly 20 to 25 minutes, the charcoal will be ready (the coals should be lightly grayed over). Using gloves, dump the charcoal into the charcoal basket or charcoal grate to completely cover the surface. If you need to move hot coals around to fill the grate area, use a pair of long-handled tongs. When the coals are spread evenly, place the cooking grate over the coals and open the air vents on the grill. The vents are usually under the grill or on the side and allow air and oxygen in to feed the fire. Place the lid on the grill and open the top vents to allow heat and smoke to escape. You might notice some whitish-gray smoke initially, but within a few minutes, it should turn either light blue or clear.

Two-Zone Setup

For a two-zone setup, you will either place a disposable aluminum pan on one side of the charcoal basket and pour hot coals on the other side of the pan or set the pan in the center of the charcoal grate and place hot coals on either side of the pan to create both direct and indirect cooking surfaces.

CHARCOAL VS. BRIQUETTES

Both lump charcoal and briquettes have their pros and cons. Briquettes tend to burn more consistently throughout the cook time than lump charcoal. Lump charcoal leaves very little ash compared to briquettes and contains no binders or fillers. Both are capable of attaining very high heat and long cook times. Some studies have shown that briquettes tend to burn slightly longer than lump charcoal. I have used both with success in my backyard and on the competition circuit. I like using lump charcoal in my barrel smokers, as the larger pieces tend to allow for better airflow and let the heat and smoke circulate throughout the chamber. When it comes to my trusty charcoal grill, I prefer using briquettes for a nice hot sear. With either fuel source, the main thing I look for is that it's made by a quality kiln or well-known brand. I also avoid any charcoal that has an added accelerant. These accelerants help ignite the charcoal, but they sometimes leave a bitter taste on your food.

FOR A GAS GRILL

Depending on the type of gas grill you have, you will want to check how the manufacturer suggests lighting your grill. Typically, there will be a valve to turn the gas on. Open the gas valve and set the grill burners to light or start. Push the ignition switch. When the grill is lit, set the burners to your desired cooking temperature. Most gas grills have a temperature gauge on the lid. You will have to adjust the burners up or down to set your cooking temperature.

Two-Zone Setup

Setting up a two-zone cooking area on your gas grill is much like the charcoal grill two-zone setup. After the grill is lit and all burners are going, shut off one side of the burners or the center burner, leaving half the burners on one side lit or, if you're using the center as a cool zone, keep on only the right and left burners.

LID UP OR DOWN?

When lighting and using a gas grill, it is paramount that the lid stays closed as much as possible. With the lid up you run the risk of the jets or burners getting blown out; if this happens, propane can pool in the bottom of the grill, which could ignite and lead to an explosion. When lighting my charcoal grill, I leave the lid off. I light the coals on the charcoal grates and set the lid off to the side until the grill is set up properly for direct or indirect cooking. When the grill is set up, place the lid on the grill, open the top vents, and adjust the bottom air vents to reach your desired cooking temperature.

SMOKING LIKE A PRO

Ah, the taste of smoky, juicy, and fatty barbecue smoked low and slow over coals and wood! There is nothing like it. It is unique and the smell draws you in. Smoke flavor can be light and smooth, or aggressive and taste like a campfire. Much like salt and pepper, smoke should be used as an ingredient to flavor and accent your food, not overpower it. Smoke can be added to your food whether cooking low and slow or hot and fast with direct grilling. In either case you will want to make sure the fire is clean and the smoke is clear or a light bluish color.

THE WOOD

There are many options when deciding how you would like to add smoke flavor to your food. Wood chips, food-grade wood pellets, and wood chunks are the most common for backyard cooking. Not only are there many options for the wood but there also are numerous options for the type or "flavor" of wood available. Sometimes it can be confusing to know which one to use for which style of cooking or cut of meat. Let's break down the available options.

Wood Chips vs. Wood Chunks

Think of this comparison as hot and fast versus low and slow. Wood chips are smaller and less dense; therefore, they will combust and burn at a faster rate. Chunks, on the other hand, are larger and denser and burn slower, making them more suitable for low-and-slow cooking.

Food-Grade Wood Pellets

Not all food-grade wood pellets are made the same. Some contain binders, fillers, and even "flavored oils." Make sure to use pellets that are all-natural and burn clean. Just because pellets are on sale doesn't mean you should buy them.

Types of Wood

There are so many types of wood that are amazing for barbecue, from Australian ironbark to South American quebracho hardwood. I am going to touch on a few of the most common and readily available at your local hardware or barbecue store.

ALDER	Subtle smoke, sweet	Beef, poultry, fish, baked goods, vegetables, game
APPLE	Light smoke, sweet	Beef, pork, poultry, baked goods, vegetables
CHARCOAL	Smoky, charcoal	Beef, poultry, vegetables, game
CHERRY	Light smoke, sweet	Pork, poultry, baked goods, vegetables
COMPETITION BLENDS	Smoky, sweet	Everything
HICKORY	Heavy smoke, woodsy	All meats, nuts, fish, cheese, vegetables
MAPLE	Mild smoke	Pork, poultry, fish, baked goods, vegetables, game
MESQUITE	Heavy smoke, creosote	Beef, poultry, fish, cheese, game
OAK	Light smoke	Beef, fish, game
PECAN	Light smoke, nutty	Beef, pork, poultry, baked goods, vegetables
WALNUT	Smoky, earthy	Beef, lamb, vegetables

SMOKING ON A CHARCOAL GRILL

Now that we have your grill set up, let's talk about adding the wood and smoke flavor. If I'm going to run an indirect, two-zone setup for lower temperature and a slower cooking process, I like to add one or two chunks of pecan wood about half the size of my fist. I place them directly on the hot coals, spread apart, about 15 to 20 minutes before I put the food on the grill. This allows time for the wood chunks to ignite and burn cleanly before my food goes on the grill. If I am cooking longer than four hours, I may add an additional chunk or two for more smoke. If I plan to cook direct, with my food right over the fire, I like to add a handful of wood chips spread throughout the hot coals just a minute or so before my food goes on the grill. The chips will ignite quickly on a hot fire and burn for only a few minutes.

KEEP IT DRY

In the barbecue classes I teach, I get asked a lot about soaking your wood chips or chunks in water, beer, wine, etc., before adding them to the fire or coals. I like to run a clean, hot fire with good airflow and add dry wood chunks or chips for flavor. Any moisture in the wood will make the fire smolder, causing unclean smoke in the grill that can possibly get on your food. The moisture can also tamp down the hot coals in a charcoal grill and cause temperature swings. Dry, aged wood is my preference when cooking indirect or direct. Save the beer and wine for happy hour.

SMOKING ON A GAS GRILL

Getting smoke flavor from a gas grill is as easy as it is on a charcoal grill. Set up your gas grill for indirect, two-zone cooking (see page 4). Once the grill has reached your desired cooking temperature, you can introduce smoke into the grill in various ways. The easiest is by adding one or two dry wood chunks half the size of your fist directly over the lit burners and letting them burn for 15 to 20 minutes before adding food to the opposite (indirect) side. You can also use a smoke box, smoke packets, or smoke tubes, all of which are easily found at most hardware and barbecue stores.

Smoke Box

A smoke box is a small box that opens on top and allows you to add wood chips or food-grade wood pellets. Sometimes they may need to be lit or ignited before being added to your grill. If the smoke box has air holes on the bottom, you can place a corner of it over the lit burner(s) to allow it to ignite and burn throughout your cook.

Smoke Packets

Smoke packets are easily made using a sheet or two of heavy-duty aluminum foil. Fold the foil into a packet the size of a small envelope (5 by 5 inches). Add a handful of your desired wood chips to the packet and fold to close it. Poke holes in the foil all over the packet, place it over the lit burner (direct side), and give it 15 to 20 minutes to ignite and start a clean smoke.

Smoke Tubes

Smoke tubes are cylindrical-shaped containers with holes throughout that you fill with food-grade wood pellets. The open end is usually lit or ignited before it's added to the grill chamber, then it's placed in the back of the grill on the indirect side. If it is not lit, add it to the back of the grill on the direct side to allow it to ignite and start smoking throughout the cook. I like to place smoke tubes in the chamber 15 to 20 minutes before adding any food to make sure it is burning clean.

THE IMPORTANCE OF MOISTURE

In order to get smoke flavor to penetrate your food, you need moisture. Smoke molecules stick to the moist or wet surface of the food you are cooking and are dissolved into the proteins. You may notice a pink or red "ring" under the outside bark (crust) on the meat. No need to worry; this is called a smoke ring and will be discussed later.

There are several ways to introduce moisture in your grill; here are a few options.

Include a water/drip pan.

When you set up your charcoal grill for two-zone cooking, you will place a disposable aluminum pan on one side or in the center. Add enough water to the pan to provide steam throughout the cook, which will add moisture into the grill chamber. If you are using a gas grill, you can place the water pan in the back on the burner or direct side.

Spray your food or apply a mop.

I often have a food-safe spray bottle filled with water or a butter-flavored vegetable oil spray (like I Can't Believe It's Not Butter) by my grill. I use it to keep my food from drying out in areas and to add moisture to the surface of the food. Wet mops can be applied as well throughout the cook, although this method will lead to a softer exterior, so if you want a good crusty bark, I would avoid it.

Salt your meat.
When salt is applied to meat, a chemical reaction occurs in which the salt attracts and draws out the natural moisture in the meat proteins. This moisture then accumulates on the surface of the meat, which will look like it is "sweating." This reaction takes time, so make sure to allow 30 minutes to an hour at room temperature after salting your meat for this to occur.

MAINTAINING TEMPERATURE

There are a few key elements to great barbecue. Maintaining a consistent temperature is one of them. When using your grill for indirect cooking, look for the grill temperature to be in the 275°F to 350°F range. You will need to adjust the air intake vents until you reach the desired temperature by opening the vents to allow air in and feed the fire, or closing the vents partially to decrease the airflow and bring the heat down. There are also several forced draft air products on the market that will regulate the grill temperature and take the guesswork out of fiddling with the vents. I recommend the BBQ Guru systems and use them on my grills. For longer cooks, I add a heaping bed of unlit lump charcoal to the charcoal basket or grate opposite the drip pan. When dumping the hot coals, I place them so they're overlapping the unlit charcoal, then adjust the vents to my desired temperature. Over time the hot coals will light the unlit coals and allow you a longer cook time.

HOW MUCH SMOKE IS ENOUGH?

As I've said, smoke should be used much like salt and pepper. It should complement the food you are cooking, not overpower its natural flavor. Most food you cook is going to accept the majority of the smoke flavor in the first few hours of the cook time. It does not need to be introduced continuously during longer cooks. I add a couple of wood chunks in the beginning of the cook, and for longer durations I will add a small chunk or two after an hour of cook time. Oversmoking can lead to creosote buildup on your food, and it may have a bitter taste. Sometimes less is more, and with smoke, this is definitely true.

GET YOUR SEAR ON (HOT AND FAST)

It's all about the sizzle with direct grilling. A hot sear is the only way to get that dark brown caramelization. This color is a result of the Maillard reaction, a complex chemical reaction that happens when proteins and sugars in food are introduced to heat, creating a crust and flavor you can get only from hot-and-fast cooking. It's hard to beat a seared steak cooked to perfection.

FIRE IT UP

For a proper sear, you will need a hot fire. While cooking low and slow, you want to stay at or under 350°F. With direct grilling, however, you are looking for 550°F to 650°F on the grate. Fire needs just a few things—oxygen, heat, and fuel. The more fuel and oxygen you give a fire, the larger or hotter it will grow, and vice versa.

KEEP IT DRY

Moisture on the surface of the meat inhibits the Maillard reaction and slows the process of achieving a good sear. For this reason, you'll want to wipe or pat dry the surface area of the meat before placing it on the hot grill for better caramelization and crust formation.

THE REVERSE SEAR

You may have seen recipes or cooking techniques calling for a reverse sear. This process involves a two-zone setup where the protein is smoked or cooked on the indirect side until it achieves or comes close to the desired internal temperature. After it reaches the proper internal temperature, the protein is placed on the direct side (over the coals) to caramelize and crust up the surface area. This process is done mostly with larger or thicker cuts of meat, like tri-tip. Because tri-tip is a dense and thick muscle, it will take some time to reach an internal temperature suitable for consumption. Bringing the internal temperature up before searing it allows you to build a nice, even crust without burning or charring the meat.

TECHNIQUES TO TASTINESS: BRINGING THE FLAVOR

There are several ways to add flavor deep down into the meat. The best one is to start with a high-quality piece of meat with a lot of intramuscular fat, or marbling—this is the fat strands you see running through the meat grains. As the meat cooks, the intramuscular fat renders, or melts down, providing flavor and moisture. The fat you see around or on the outside of the meat is mostly intermuscular fat, which will not render into the proteins. Besides starting with a quality piece of meat, there are also other ways to add flavor.

SPATCHCOCKING

Spatchcocking refers to a process in which the backbone is removed from a whole chicken, turkey, or other game bird to open the cavity and create a more even surface area for seasonings and smoke to reach. The process involves cutting both sides parallel to the backbone to remove it using kitchen shears or a sharp knife, then pressing down to break the breastbone so the bird lies flat on the grill.

BRINING

Brining is the process of submerging your meat in a saltwater solution. This process allows the proteins to retain more moisture and adds flavor deep into the meat, while the salt tenderizes the proteins, making it juicier and softer. You can use a wet brine or a dry brine.

Wet Brine

As the name suggests, wet brining uses a mixture of water and salt, sugar, or other flavorings like herbs, citrus juices, and beer. The solution is boiled or heated, then cooled before the meat is added. Brining is often done for several hours or overnight. After brining, the meat is usually rinsed in cold water to remove any excess salt or seasoning, then dried.

Dry Brine

The dry brining process uses no water. Salt and sometimes other seasonings are added directly to the meat proteins, and over time the salt draws out the natural moisture in the meat to its surface. The natural juices then mix with the salt and seasoning and reabsorb back into the meat protein. This process can take several hours as well, but it's well worth the time.

FLAVOR INJECTIONS

I like to use injections to add more flavor and moisture deep into meat proteins, especially when I am competing. We have limited time before we turn in our entries for judging, so injecting the meat adds flavor and moisture within a short amount of time. When I cook in my backyard I rarely inject, because I have time to properly prepare and season my food.

TEXAS CRUTCH

The term *Texas crutch* refers to wrapping your larger cuts of meat, traditionally brisket, in aluminum foil or unwaxed butcher paper partway through the cooking process. This is usually done once the bark or surface crust has set and is dry to the touch. The brisket is removed from the grill, tightly wrapped (sometimes along with beef broth, consommé, butter, or other flavorings), then placed back on the grill to continue cooking until tender. Wrapping your meat retains moisture and adds flavor as the meat braises in its own juices and other added ingredients. When cooking larger cuts of meat low and slow, you may notice that at some point the internal temperature doesn't seem to change or even decrease for a few hours. This is called the "stall" and has left many backyard cooks baffled. No need to worry—all you need to push through the stall are time and heat. Using the Texas crutch method helps push through the stall faster, as the radiant heat and liquid will cause the meat to cook faster wrapped than unwrapped.

HOW TO KNOW IT'S DONE

This is where it all comes together. You have spent time seasoning the food correctly, getting the fire set up, and cooking your food; now it's time to eat. But is it done? The number one question I get asked in the classes I teach is "How long do I cook it?" I always answer, "Until it's done!" To know when it's "done," you first need to have a goal of what you want to accomplish with that specific dish, as well as how you or your guests like their food cooked.

DIFFERENT KINDS OF DONE

Certain cuts of meat are best served and eaten at lower internal temperatures than other cuts. Steaks, tenderloins, and roasts like tri-tip tend to retain the most flavor and have the best texture when cooked medium-rare to medium, with an internal temperature between 130°F and 140°F. Brisket, ribs, and pork shoulder, on the other hand, are best at a much higher internal temperature, usually 205°F and beyond. At this temperature, the meat will be super tender and almost shred apart. The high heat is needed on those cuts to break down the denser muscle fibers, connective tissues, and intermuscular fat between muscle groups. The US Department of Agriculture (USDA) also sets safety standards for safe minimum cooking temperatures for most proteins. The minimum safe internal temperature is 165°F for poultry and most seafood, and 145°F for pork. That being said, just because the food is safe to consume doesn't mean it's done.

CARRYOVER HEAT AND RESTING

Once the meat has reached the proper internal temperature and texture you are looking for, remove it from the grill promptly. While on the grill, the meat builds heat internally, and this heat will continue to rise even after the meat has been removed from the grill. This "carryover heat" can sometimes push your proteins into the overdone stage, and it can take large cuts from perfectly tender with structure to mushy and soft. This is where resting and holding come into play. Depending on the cut of meat and how long it was cooked, resting can last between a few minutes and hours. Beef brisket cooked low and slow can rest and be held for over 8 hours, whereas a chicken breast may need only 10 to 15 minutes. Resting allows the juices to settle and redistribute throughout the meat, which leads to more moisture. I like to let pretty much everything I cook rest before slicing and serving. I find it leads to a better finished product.

THE SMOKE RING

We touched on the smoke ring earlier when we were talking about moisture. A smoke ring is a reddish-pink band that surrounds the surface of smoked meats. It is formed by smoke molecules attaching to water molecules on the surface of the meat and interacting with myoglobin, a reddish-colored protein within the meat. It is important to know what the smoke ring is, as some of your guests may think the meat is raw on the outside and cooked in the center. You can assure them that is not the case, and what they are seeing is a properly smoked piece of meat.

A CLEAN GRILL IS A HAPPY GRILL

When I was deployed on my ship during my service in the US Navy, the ship captain would say, "If cleanliness is next to godliness, then this ship is going to be the holiest ship in the fleet." I treat my grills the same way. Proper cleaning habits and grill maintenance are invaluable to get the best product from your grill. Ash and grease buildup, dirty cooking grates, and creosote can ruin all the hard work you put into making the best product for your friends and family. I clean my grills before each use and make sure the cooking grates are brushed down and clean after each use.

THE RECIPES

The recipes I share in this book are meant to be a guide and a resource to help you cook almost any type of protein or cut of meat on your grill or smoker. I am including traditional tried-and-true backyard staples as well as recipes I have picked up during my global barbecue adventures. You'll also find some of my favorite recipes and a few from my barbecue friends, some of the best pitmasters in the business. Everything from prep and cook times to suggested wood type will be covered. I have also included variations to some recipes to change things up and some Pro Tips to take your barbecue to the next level. I don't know about you, but I'm ready to cook—let's get started!

A note on seasoning: When seasoning proteins and vegetables, pay attention to the structure and mass of the protein. For example, a light coat of seasoning on a 6-ounce chicken breast may be about 1 tablespoon of seasoning as opposed to a light coat of seasoning on a 15-pound brisket, which may be about ¼ cup. Also, brisket, being a dense, large cut of meat, may require a heavy coat of seasoning.

I use light seasoning on poultry and seafood and season more liberally on large cuts of meat like brisket, pork shoulder, and ribs. For the purposes of keeping things simple, each recipe calls for a specific amount (or range) of seasoning. Feel free to adjust these based on your personal preference. Also, keep in mind that you may have seasoning left over for some recipes—this is totally okay. Just discard the excess.

APPETIZERS

◀ Chicken Wings with
White BBQ Sauce (page 23)

PORK BELLY PIMENTO CHEESE BITES

SERVES 10 TO 12 / PREP TIME: 30 to 45 minutes / **COOK TIME:** 3 to 3½ hours
SUGGESTED WOOD: Pecan wood chunks

I made these for one of my barbecue appetizer classes, and they were a huge hit. The sweet and savory pork belly pairs perfectly with the rich and creamy pimento cheese. These are sure to be a crowd-pleaser at your next gathering. Also, the pimento cheese dip is fantastic all by itself or with crackers and vegetables.

For the pimento cheese

8 ounces cream cheese, softened
2 cups shredded cheddar cheese (from an 8-ounce block)
½ cup mayonnaise, preferably Duke's
1 (4-ounce) jar pimentos, drained and diced
1 jalapeño pepper, diced
½ teaspoon cayenne pepper
¼ teaspoon ancho chile powder
¼ teaspoon garlic powder
¼ teaspoon onion powder
Pinch salt ▸

1. **TO MAKE THE PIMENTO CHEESE:** Mix all the ingredients in a bowl until combined thoroughly. Cover and chill in the refrigerator until needed.

2. **TO MAKE THE PORK BELLY:** Trim the pork belly of any excess fat and score the fat side in a diamond pattern about ¼ inch deep.

3. Season all sides of the belly with the rub and set aside.

4. Set up your grill for indirect cooking (see page 4). Fill a charcoal chimney with lump charcoal and light it with a fire starter cube. When the coals have turned gray, dump them into the grill on the side opposite the disposable aluminum pan, replace the cooking grate, close the lid, and open the top and bottom vents until the grill temperature registers about 275°F. Continue to monitor the grill, adjusting the vents as needed, until it reaches a cooking temperature of 300°F to 325°F. About 15 minutes before you plan to cook, place 1 or 2 medium pecan wood chunks directly on the hot coals, then close the lid.

5. Place the pork belly fat-side up on the grate directly over the drip pan, close the lid, and cook for 1 hour. Flip the pork belly over, rotate it, and cook for another 1 to 1½ hours, until the bark (crust) is set.

For the pork belly

1 (4- to 5-pound) pork belly, skin removed

3 to 4 tablespoons Sweet and Savory Rub (page 195)

½ cup apple juice

½ to ¾ cup Southwest Sweet Heat BBQ Sauce (page 199), divided

1 jalapeño, sliced, seeded if desired

6. Remove the pork belly from the grill and let it rest for 20 minutes. Cut the pork belly into 1½-inch cubes and place them in another disposable aluminum pan with the apple juice. Pour ½ cup of barbecue sauce over the pork and toss, then cover the pan with aluminum foil. At this time, if the fire needs more fuel, add half a chimney of unlit charcoal to the hot portion.

7. Place the pan back on the indirect side of the grill, maintaining a temperature of 300°F to 325°F. Cook for another hour, then test the tenderness of the pork belly by opening the foil and using the tip of your thermometer to probe into a couple of the cubes. The probe should slide into the meat with little to no resistance, and the internal temperature should be at least 200°F.

8. When the pork belly cubes are done, remove the pan from the grill and let rest for 10 minutes. Remove the pimento cheese from the refrigerator and set aside.

9. After a 10-minute rest, coat the pork belly cubes in the pan sauce. If you want more sauce, add another ¼ cup of barbecue sauce to the pan. Place the cubes on a serving plate, top each with a spoonful of pimento cheese and a jalapeño slice, and serve.

PRO TIP: In the first stages of cooking the pork belly, make sure to keep a lookout for edges getting dry or crumbly. I always keep a spray bottle filled with water or butter-flavored vegetable oil handy in case I need to moisten the pork.

CRAB- AND SAUSAGE-STUFFED MUSHROOM CAPS

SERVES 10 TO 12 / **PREP TIME:** 30 to 45 minutes / **COOK TIME:** 25 to 35 minutes
SUGGESTED WOOD: Applewood chunks

The combination of crab and sausage in these mushroom caps is a flavor bomb. You can also use portobello mushrooms and change up the filling—try using cooked shrimp and leftover brisket.

10 to 12 medium white mushroom caps, cleaned, stems removed and discarded
Avocado oil spray
1 cup lump crabmeat
½ cup crumbled cooked breakfast sausage
8 ounces cream cheese, softened
¼ cup dried bread crumbs
¼ cup grated Parmesan cheese, divided
¼ cup chopped fresh Italian parsley
¼ cup diced scallions, divided
½ teaspoon garlic powder
Pinch salt
Pinch freshly ground black pepper

1. Set up your grill for indirect cooking (see page 4). Fill a charcoal chimney with lump charcoal and light it with a fire starter cube. When the coals have turned gray, dump them into the grill on the side opposite the disposable aluminum pan, replace the cooking grate, then close the lid and adjust the vents until the grill reaches a cooking temperature of 300°F to 325°F. About 15 minutes before you plan to cook, place 1 or 2 small applewood chunks directly on the hot coals, then close the lid.

2. Place the mushroom caps in a disposable aluminum half-size pan, spray them with avocado oil, and grill for 5 to 10 minutes. Set aside.

3. In a large mixing bowl, combine the remaining ingredients, reserving 1 tablespoon each of Parmesan cheese and scallions, until fully incorporated.

4. Scoop about 1 heaping tablespoon of filling into each mushroom cap, then top with the reserved 1 tablespoon Parmesan. Place the pan back on the indirect side of the grill, maintaining a temperature of 300°F to 325°F.

5. Cook for 20 to 25 minutes, rotating the pan halfway through, until the cheese is melted. Remove from the grill, top with the reserved 1 tablespoon diced scallions, and serve.

LOADED SKILLET QUESO DIP

SERVES 10 TO 12 / **PREP TIME:** 15 to 30 minutes / **COOK TIME:** 30 to 45 minutes
SUGGESTED WOOD: Applewood chunks

This skillet dip has become a favorite in my family, and it is super easy to make. It is the perfect appetizer for using up that leftover pulled pork or brisket you have in the refrigerator. You can easily prepare this ahead of time and refrigerate it until you're ready to light the grill.

1 (32-ounce) block
Velveeta cheese, cut
into cubes

1 cup leftover cooked
brisket, pulled pork, or
shredded chicken

1 jalapeño, diced, seeded
if desired

1 cup shredded Monterey
Jack cheese

1 (10-ounce) can diced
tomatoes and green
chiles, such as
Rotel, drained

1 (15-ounce) can black
beans, drained
and rinsed

½ cup sour cream

¼ cup chopped fresh
cilantro

Tortilla chips and/
or sliced veggies,
for serving

1. Set up your grill for indirect cooking (see page 4). Fill a charcoal chimney with lump charcoal and light it with a fire starter cube. When the coals have turned gray, dump them into the grill on the side opposite the disposable aluminum pan, replace the cooking grate, close the lid, and adjust the vents until the grill reaches a cooking temperature of 275°F to 300°F. About 15 minutes before you plan to cook, place 1 or 2 small applewood chunks directly on the hot coals, then close the lid.

2. Combine all the ingredients except the cilantro and tortilla chips/veggies in another disposable aluminum pan or cast-iron skillet and mix them together.

3. Place the pan on the indirect side of the grill and cook for 15 minutes.

4. After 15 minutes, rotate the pan and stir the mixture. Cook another 15 minutes, then rotate the pan and stir again. You want the cheese to be smooth without any lumps; cook another 15 minutes if it's not lump-free and melted. Remove from the grill.

5. Top with the chopped cilantro and serve with tortilla chips and/or sliced veggies.

PROSCIUTTO-WRAPPED MASCARPONE-STUFFED DATES

MAKES 12 TO 16 DATES / **PREP TIME:** 15 to 30 minutes / **COOK TIME:** 20 to 25 minutes
SUGGESTED WOOD: Maple wood chunk

This is my wife's favorite appetizer not only to eat but also to make. The sweetness from the dates and the honey paired with the salty prosciutto is a sweet-and-salty lover's dream.

½ cup mascarpone
cheese, softened

3 tablespoons honey, plus
more for drizzling

3 tablespoons finely
chopped pecans, plus
more for serving

Pinch salt

12 to 16 large Medjool
dates, sliced lengthwise
and pits removed

6 to 8 thin slices
prosciutto

1. Set up your grill for indirect cooking (see page 4). Fill a charcoal chimney with lump charcoal and light it with a fire starter cube. When the coals have turned gray, dump them into the grill on the side opposite the disposable aluminum pan, replace the cooking grate, close the lid, and open the top and bottom vents until the grill temperature registers about 275°F. Continue to monitor the grill, adjusting the vents as needed, until it reaches a cooking temperature of 300°F to 325°F. About 15 minutes before you plan to cook, place a small maple wood chunk directly on the hot coals, then close the lid.

2. In a mixing bowl, combine the mascarpone cheese, honey, chopped pecans, and salt, stirring to blend well.

3. Evenly fill the cavity of each date with the mascarpone cheese mixture.

4. Slice the prosciutto into 1-inch-wide strips and wrap each date with one, securing it with a toothpick.

5. Place the dates on the indirect side of the grill and cook for 20 to 25 minutes, until the prosciutto starts curling and gets a little crusty. When the dates are done, remove them to a serving tray. Garnish with a drizzle of honey and extra chopped pecans, then serve.

Chicken Wings with White BBQ Sauce

SERVES 4 TO 6 / PREP TIME: 4 to 6 hours / **COOK TIME:** 45 minutes to 1 hour
SUGGESTED WOOD: Cherrywood chunks

These wings are inspired by my good friend Chef Dom Ruggiero. He serves them in his restaurant, and I fell in love with the combination of the white sauce with peanuts. Initially I was intrigued, but after the first bite I wanted more. This classic white sauce pairs well with poultry as well as beef, pork, and seafood.

12 fully jointed chicken wings

1 (16-ounce) bottle Italian dressing

1 teaspoon salt

1 teaspoon freshly ground black pepper

½ teaspoon cayenne pepper

Butter-flavored vegetable oil spray

1 recipe Classic White BBQ Sauce (page 200)

¼ cup chopped peanuts

¼ cup thinly sliced scallions

1. Pat the chicken wings dry using paper towels. With a fork, puncture holes all over each wing. Place them in a large resealable plastic bag or a glass bowl and pour the Italian dressing over the wings. Toss, cover, and refrigerate for 4 to 6 hours.

2. Set up your grill for indirect cooking (see page 4). Fill a charcoal chimney with lump charcoal and light it with a fire starter cube. When the coals have turned gray, dump them into the grill on the side opposite the disposable aluminum pan, replace the cooking grate, close the lid, and open the top and bottom vents until the grill temperature registers about 275°F. Continue to monitor the grill, adjusting the vents as needed, until it reaches a cooking temperature of 300°F to 325°F. About 15 minutes before you plan to cook, place 1 or 2 small cherrywood chunks directly on the hot coals, then close the lid.

3. Remove the wings from the marinade and pat them dry with paper towels. Season with the salt, black pepper, and cayenne.

CONTINUED

4. When the grill is ready, place the wings on the indirect side over the drip pan and cook for 20 minutes. If the wings are looking crusty, spray them with butter spray and rotate. Cook for another 20 minutes, then spray again, if necessary.

5. After 40 minutes the wings should be close to done (the internal temperature needs to be at least 165°F). Remove them from the grill and let rest for 5 minutes. While the wings are resting, warm up the white barbecue sauce.

6. Dunk each wing in the sauce and place them on a serving tray. Top with the chopped peanuts and scallions. Serve with extra sauce on the side.

PRO TIP: Even though the safe internal temperature for chicken is 165°F, I like my chicken wings between 180°F and 190°F. The higher temperature and longer cook time helps make them more tender, while rendering the fat under the skin.

SMOKED RAINBOW TROUT DIP

SERVES 6 / **PREP TIME:** 8 hours to overnight / **COOK TIME:** 1 hour
SUGGESTED WOOD: Pecan wood chunks

This is another recipe I first tried at chef Dom Ruggiero's restaurant. I loved it so much that I asked him to share the recipe in a cooking video we shot together. This is my version of his recipe, adapted for the grill.

3 or 4 (6-ounce) rainbow trout fillets, deboned, skin on or off

1 gallon Poultry and Seafood Herb Brine (page 202)

½ cup mascarpone cheese, softened

½ cup chopped fresh chives, plus extra for serving

4 ounces cream cheese, softened

1 cup sour cream

2 tablespoons prepared horseradish

2 tablespoons freshly squeezed lemon juice

2 tablespoons chopped fresh dill

Saltine crackers and sliced vegetables, for serving

1. Place the trout fillets in a large resealable bag or a bowl, then add the brine, cover, and refrigerate for at least 8 hours or overnight.

2. Remove the fillets from the brine and discard the liquid. Pat the fillets dry with paper towels and lay them flat on a wire rack. Let them come to room temperature for 30 to 45 minutes, until they start to sweat and form a pellicle, which is a thin film that develops as the fish rests.

3. Set up your grill for indirect cooking (see page 4). Fill a charcoal chimney with lump charcoal and light it with a fire starter cube. When the coals have turned gray, dump them into the grill on the side opposite the disposable aluminum pan, replace the cooking grate, close the lid, and open the top and bottom vents until the grill registers about 150°F. Continue to monitor the grill, adjusting the vents as needed, until it reaches a cooking temperature of 200°F to 225°F. About 15 minutes before you plan to cook, place 1 or 2 small pecan wood chunks directly on the hot coals, then close the lid.

CONTINUED

4. When the grill is ready, place the fillets on the indirect side of the grill over the drip pan. Cook for 1 hour, or until they reach an internal temperature of 145°F and start to flake. Remove them from the grill and set aside on a platter.

5. In a large mixing bowl, combine the mascarpone, chives, cream cheese, sour cream, horseradish, lemon juice, and dill, mixing to blend well.

6. When the fish has cooled, crumble it into small pieces with your fingers, making sure to remove any pin bones that may have been left behind. Fold the crumbled fish into the mascarpone mixture and stir gently to combine.

7. Sprinkle the dip with extra chives and serve with saltine crackers and sliced veggies.

PRO TIP: Letting the pellicle form on the fish allows it to attract more smoke. Be sure to allow time for the fish to start sweating and form this liquidy layer before putting it on the grill.

Spicy Candied Bacon

SERVES 4 TO 6 / **PREP TIME:** 30 minutes / **COOK TIME:** 45 to 50 minutes
SUGGESTED WOOD: Maple wood chunks

The recipe calls for a package of bacon, but I suggest you double it. These strips will be gone before you know it. My kids love these as toppings on their burgers, and I love them crumbled in salads, macaroni and cheese, popcorn—and many other things! Try them covered in chocolate for a salty-sweet treat.

1 (12-ounce) package
thick-cut bacon
1 cup packed light
brown sugar
1 tablespoon salt
1 tablespoon freshly
ground black pepper
1 tablespoon ancho
chile powder

1. Lay the bacon strips on a wire rack set over a foil-lined baking sheet.

2. In a small mixing bowl, combine the brown sugar, salt, pepper, and ancho chile powder. Using half this mixture, sprinkle it evenly on each slice of bacon and let them sit at room temperature for 10 to 15 minutes, until the brown sugar melts into the bacon.

3. Flip the bacon strips and sprinkle the remaining mixture on the other side, letting them sit at room temperature for another 10 to 15 minutes.

4. Set up your grill for indirect cooking (see page 4). Fill a charcoal chimney with lump charcoal and light it with a fire starter cube. When the coals have turned gray, dump them into the grill on the side opposite the disposable aluminum pan, replace the cooking grate, close the lid, and open the top and bottom vents until the grill registers about 250°F. Continue to monitor the grill, adjusting the vents as needed, until it reaches a cooking temperature of 275°F to 300°F. About 15 minutes before you plan to cook, place 1 or 2 small maple wood chunks directly on the hot coals, then close the lid.

CONTINUED

5. When the grill is ready, place the rack of bacon on the indirect side over the drip pan, close the lid, and open the vents.

6. After about 25 minutes, rotate the rack and flip the bacon pieces if they are getting too dark on one side.

7. Cook for an additional 20 to 25 minutes, until the fat caramelizes.

8. Remove from the grill and let rest for 5 to 10 minutes, then serve.

PRO TIP: If some edge pieces are getting dark on the outside of the rack, rotate them with the center pieces so they cook evenly. Don't be afraid to take off the strips that are done while continuing to cook the others.

Sausage-Wrapped Stuffed Jalapeños

SERVES 2 OR 3 / **PREP TIME:** 30 to 45 minutes / **COOK TIME:** 50 minutes to 1 hour
SUGGESTED WOOD: Hickory wood chunks

These tasty treats have gone by many names—armadillo eggs, ABTs (atomic buffalo turds), and sausage poppers are just a few. I have used ground beef, chorizo, and even javelina sausage for this recipe. Feel free to mix it up with other ground meats of your choice.

6 to 10 jalapeños
8 ounces cream cheese
¼ cup grated sharp cheddar cheese
¼ cup crumbled Spicy Candied Bacon (page 27) or leftover cooked bacon
2 tablespoons Sweet and Savory Rub (page 195), divided
1 pound breakfast sausage, crumbled
Southwest Sweet Heat BBQ Sauce (page 199), to taste

1. Cut off just the top of each jalapeño, then core and seed them with a butter knife. Set aside.

2. In a large bowl, combine the cream cheese, cheddar cheese, crumbled bacon, and 1 tablespoon of the rub until thoroughly incorporated.

3. Fill each jalapeño with some of the cream cheese mixture.

4. Evenly divide the breakfast sausage into as many portions as you have jalapeños. Evenly cover each stuffed jalapeño with one portion of the sausage; it will have an egg-like shape (hence the name "armadillo eggs"). Sprinkle each "egg" with the remaining rub and set them aside.

5. Set up your grill for indirect cooking (see page 4). Fill a charcoal chimney with lump charcoal and light it with a fire starter cube. When the coals have turned gray, dump them into the grill on the side opposite the disposable aluminum pan, replace the cooking grate, close the lid, and open the top and bottom vents until the grill temperature registers about 275°F. Continue to monitor the grill, adjusting the vents as needed, until it reaches a cooking temperature of 300°F to 325°F. About 15 minutes before you plan to cook, place 1 or 2 small hickory wood chunks directly on the hot coals, then close the lid.

CONTINUED

6. When the grill is ready, place the "eggs" on the indirect side over the drip pan, close the lid, and open the vents.

7. After 20 to 25 minutes, flip the eggs if they are getting too dark on one side. Cook for an additional 20 to 25 minutes, until they are a nice mahogany color, then brush each egg with barbecue sauce. Cook for another 10 minutes, then remove the eggs from the grill and let rest for 10 minutes.

8. Slice each egg crosswise into medallions, place them on a serving tray, and enjoy.

PRO TIP: If you have any leftover brisket or pulled pork, add some to the cream cheese mixture for another level of flavor. If you have any cream cheese mixture left after filling the jalapeños, save it for topping baked potatoes or mix it in with mashed potatoes.

CHARRED ONION SLIDERS

MAKES 12 SLIDERS / **PREP TIME:** 30 to 45 minutes / **COOK TIME:** 10 to 15 minutes
SUGGESTED WOOD: Pecan wood chips

Who doesn't love sliders? These little bite-size burgers are oniony and cheesy, and they'll have you reaching for seconds and thirds. This recipe works best with a flat-top grill. You can easily turn your grill into a flat top by adding a product called GrillGrates. I love these grates and use them for most of my cooking at home. They can be flipped over to create a flat surface on your grill and used for many other cooking applications.

2 pounds 80/20
    ground beef
2 tablespoons SPGJ Rub
    (page 194)
Avocado oil spray
1 or 2 large Vidalia or
    sweet onions, sliced
    into ¼-inch-thick rings
12 slices cheddar cheese
12 slider buns
Spicy Dijon mustard,
    for topping
Bread-and-butter pickle
    slices, for topping

1. Form the ground beef into 12 equal-size patties.

2. Season both sides of each patty with the rub, then spray both sides with avocado oil and set aside.

3. Set up your grill for direct cooking (see page 3). Fill a charcoal chimney with charcoal and light it with a fire starter cube. When the coals have turned gray, dump them into the grill grate or basket in an even layer, place a flat-top grill grate (if using) on the cooking grate, close the lid, and open the top and bottom vents. Right before you plan to cook, scatter a small handful of pecan wood chips directly on the hot coals.

4. Season the onion slices with the rub and spray both sides with avocado oil.

5. Place the onions on the flat top if you are using one; if not, space them evenly all around the grill. Cook for 2 to 3 minutes, then flip them.

6. Top each onion ring with a burger patty and close the lid. Cook for 3 to 4 minutes, then flip the burger patties. Some of the onion rings may need to be flipped as well. Cook for another 2 to 3 minutes.

CONTINUED

7. When the onions are caramelized and the burgers are almost done to your preference, place a slice of cheddar cheese on each patty. Close the lid and cook for another 1 to 2 minutes, just until the cheese melts. Remove the burgers and onions from the grill and set them aside.

8. Toast the slider buns by spraying the cut sides of each with avocado oil and placing them cut-side down over the hot coals for 1 to 2 minutes, until they start to brown, then remove.

9. Build your sliders with a cheesy burger patty, spicy Dijon mustard, pickles, and lots of caramelized onions.

PRO TIP: You can use the flat-top side of the GrillGrates for many other recipes, from cheesesteaks to frying eggs and bacon. They have multiple uses and are a "grate" tool to add to your barbecue accessories.

PORTOBELLO MUSHROOM PIZZA BITES

SERVES 3 OR 4 / **PREP TIME:** 30 to 45 minutes / **COOK TIME:** 20 to 25 minutes
SUGGESTED WOOD: Applewood chunks

Portobello Mushroom Pizza Bites are an awesome appetizer, but they can also be your main dish. Use bigger mushroom caps and fill them up with your favorite toppings to make them dinner size.

6 to 8 portobello mushroom caps, about 2 inches in diameter, cleaned, stems removed and discarded

1 (15.5-ounce) jar marinara or pizza sauce

1 cup shredded mozzarella cheese

12 to 24 pepperoni slices

1 small onion, diced

1 green bell pepper, diced

½ cup sliced black olives

½ cup grated Parmesan cheese

4 or 5 basil leaves, chopped

1. Set up your grill for indirect cooking (see page 4). Fill a charcoal chimney with lump charcoal and light it with a fire starter cube. When the coals have turned gray, dump them into the grill on the side opposite the disposable aluminum pan, replace the cooking grate, close the lid, and open the top and bottom vents until the grill temperature registers about 275°F. Continue to monitor the grill, adjusting the vents as needed, until it reaches 300°F to 325°F. About 15 minutes before you plan to cook, place 1 or 2 small applewood chunks directly on the hot coals, then close the lid.

2. Lay the mushroom caps on a baking sheet and top each with marinara sauce, mozzarella, pepperoni, onion, bell pepper, and black olives (or you can switch up the toppings and use whatever you'd like).

3. When the grill is ready, place the mushroom caps on the indirect side of the grill over the drip pan and cook for 15 to 20 minutes, until the cheese melts and the mushrooms soften.

4. After the cheese melts, use tongs to place the mushroom caps directly over the coals. Sear the mushrooms for 1 to 2 minutes, making sure not to burn the bottoms.

5. Remove them from grill and let rest for 5 to 10 minutes, then top with basil and enjoy.

Chapter 3

BEEF, LAMB, AND VENISON

◀ Beer and Onion Braised Beef
Short Ribs (page 66)

TRI-TIP FRENCH DIP WITH AU JUS

SERVES 4 TO 6 / PREP TIME: 30 to 45 minutes / COOK TIME: 45 minutes to 1 hour
SUGGESTED WOOD: Pecan wood chunks

This recipe features the reverse-sear method we talked about in chapter 1. I think tri-tip is a very underrated cut of meat, and you'll find that it's even more delicious when reverse-seared. Cooked properly, a tri-tip can rival the best rib eye or filet at any top steak house. As with most beef, you want to look for a lot of marbling and a nice uniform roast.

1 (3- to 5-pound) whole
  tri-tip roast, trimmed,
  with fat cap removed
3 tablespoons SPGJ Rub
  (page 194)
1 whole sweet onion
Avocado oil spray
1 (1-ounce) packet
  au jus mix
2 tablespoons prepared
  horseradish
½ cup mayonnaise
½ teaspoon freshly
  ground black pepper
4 to 6 hoagie or sub rolls
4 to 6 slices
  provolone cheese

1. Season all sides of the tri-tip with the rub and set aside for up to 1½ hours before putting it on the grill. Slice the onion into ¼-inch-thick rings, season with the rub, spray avocado oil on both sides, and set aside.

2. Prepare the au jus as indicated on the packet and pour it into a small disposable aluminum loaf pan. In a separate bowl, combine the horseradish, mayonnaise, and pepper, stir, cover, and refrigerate until ready to use.

3. Set up your grill for indirect cooking (see page 4). Fill a charcoal chimney with lump charcoal and light it with a fire starter cube. When the coals have turned gray, dump them into the grill on the side opposite the disposable aluminum pan, replace the cooking grate, close the lid, and open the top and bottom vents until the grill temperature registers about 275°F. Continue to monitor the grill, adjusting the vents as needed, until it reaches a cooking temperature of 300°F to 325°F. About 15 minutes before you plan to cook, place 1 or 2 medium pecan wood chunks directly on the hot coals, then close the lid.

4. When the fire is running clean, place the tri-tip and the au jus pan on the indirect side over the drip pan and cook for 30 minutes, then flip and rotate the tri-tip for uniform cooking. Place the onion slices directly over the coals.

5. Cook for 5 to 10 minutes more, flip the onions, then test the internal temperature of the tri-tip using an instant-read thermometer inserted into the thickest part; I like mine to reach 125°F to 128°F. When the onions are caramelized, remove them from the grill and set aside.

6. Once the tri-tip reaches the desired temperature, remove the au jus pan and set it aside. Fully open the bottom vents to feed the fire and increase the temperature. Give the grill about 5 minutes to come up to temperature, then place the tri-tip directly over the coals to sear.

7. Cook each side for a minute or two to crust up. Remove the tri-tip when it reaches an internal temperature of about 133°F, or your desired doneness. Cover lightly with aluminum foil and let rest for 15 to 20 minutes.

8. Spray the hoagie rolls with avocado oil and toast over the coals for 1 to 2 minutes.

9. After the tri-tip has rested, lay it on a cutting board and slice it thinly across the grain.

10. To build your sandwich, slather some horseradish mayonnaise on both sides of the toasted hoagie roll. Pile some thinly sliced tri-tip on the bottom bun, then top with a slice of provolone cheese and some grilled onions. Serve with warm au jus on the side.

PRO TIP: When slicing tri-tip, pay special attention to the way the grain runs. If you cut with the grain, the slices may be tough and chewy. Slicing perpendicular to (or across) the grain will result in a more tender bite.

JIMMY'S EPIC SAUCE BURGER

SERVES 4 TO 6 / **PREP TIME:** 30 to 45 minutes / **COOK TIME:** 8 to 10 minutes
SUGGESTED WOOD: Pecan wood chips

I get asked many times which one of my barbecue "wins" is the favorite. This recipe is among my favorites, but it's not mine. My son and daughter entered a kids' burger competition at an event I was in a few years ago. The winner of the kids' competition had the honor of having their burger recipe in the Operation BBQ Relief (OBR) cookbook. My son ended up winning the event, and this is his recipe.

2 to 3 pounds
   80/20 ground beef
2 tablespoons Sweet and
   Savory Rub (page 195)
Avocado oil spray
½ cup mayonnaise
¼ cup ketchup
1 tablespoon hot sauce
2 teaspoon extra-virgin
   olive oil
4 to 6 slices
   cheddar cheese
4 to 6 hamburger buns
4 to 6 slices Spicy
   Candied Bacon (page 27)
2 Roma tomatoes,
   thinly sliced
1 to 1½ cups shredded
   iceberg lettuce

1. Divide and form the ground beef into 4 to 6 equal-size patties. Season both sides with the rub and spray with avocado oil. Set aside.

2. In a small bowl, make the Epic Sauce by combining the mayonnaise, ketchup, hot sauce, and olive oil. Stir until blended, cover, and refrigerate until ready to use.

3. Set up your grill for direct cooking (see page 3). Fill a charcoal chimney with charcoal and light it with a fire starter cube. When the coals have turned gray, dump them into the grill grate or basket in an even layer, close the lid, and open the top and bottom vents. Right before you plan to cook, scatter a small handful of pecan wood chips directly on the hot coals.

4. Open the lid, place the burger patties on the grate directly over the coals, and cook for 1½ to 2 minutes. Open the lid and give the patties a 90-degree turn. Close the lid and cook for another 1½ to 2 minutes.

5. Open the lid and flip the burgers. Cook for 1½ to 2 minutes, then open the lid and give the burgers another 90-degree turn. Place a slice of cheese on each patty and close the lid.

6. After 1 to 2 minutes, or when your desired doneness is reached, remove the burgers to a platter and let rest for 5 to 10 minutes.

7. Slather both sides of each bun with Epic Sauce. Place the burger patty on the bottom bun, add 2 slices of candied bacon, another dollop of the sauce, a few tomato slices, and shredded lettuce. Add the top bun and enjoy!

PRO TIP: Try this recipe with ground chicken, turkey, pork, or lamb. The Epic Sauce complements all types of protein.

First-Place Rack of Lamb

SERVES 4 TO 6 / **PREP TIME:** 30 to 45 minutes / **COOK TIME:** 35 to 40 minutes
SUGGESTED WOOD: Pecan wood chunks

Lamb holds a special place in my heart. In 2017 I was invited to compete in the Australian Brewery Kingsford Invitational. I was excited to be traveling Down Under to compete, but I knew the Australasian Barbecue Alliance competitions included a lamb category, which I wasn't as familiar with, so I practiced and cooked lamb for four months straight before the event. Long story short, I ended up taking first place in the lamb category and was invited back in 2018, when I took first place in the lamb category as well!

1 (1½-pound) rack of lamb, bone-in, frenched (see Pro Tip)

2 tablespoons SPGJ Rub (page 194)

8 tablespoons (1 stick) salted butter

1 rosemary sprig

2 or 3 garlic cloves, minced

1 teaspoon Worcestershire sauce

1. Trim excess fat and silver skin from the entire rack. You want to make sure the seasoning adheres to the meat, not the fat or silver skin.

2. Season the lamb with a moderate amount of the rub and set it aside at room temperature.

3. In a small disposable aluminum pan, combine the butter, rosemary, and minced garlic and set aside.

4. Set up your grill for indirect cooking (see page 4). Fill a charcoal chimney with lump charcoal and light it with a fire starter cube. When the coals have turned gray, dump them into the grill on the side opposite the disposable aluminum pan, replace the cooking grate, close the lid, and open the top and bottom vents until the grill temperature registers about 275°F. Continue to monitor the grill, adjusting the vents as needed, until it reaches a cooking temperature of 300°F to 325°F. About 15 minutes before you plan to cook, place 1 or 2 medium pecan wood chunks directly on the hot coals, then close the lid.

5. When the grill is ready, lift the lid and place the rack of lamb as well as the pan with the butter mixture on the indirect side of the grill. Close the lid and cook for 15 minutes.

6. Open the lid, rotate the lamb 180 degrees, and cook for another 10 minutes, then test the internal temperature of the lamb—you are looking for 120°F to 125°F.

7. When the rack reaches the desired temperature, baste it with the butter mixture and place it directly over the coals. Cook for 1 to 2 minutes, basting once. Flip the rack over and cook for another 1 to 2 minutes, basting it again. Cook and baste until the internal temperature of the lamb reaches 135°F to 138°F, or your preferred doneness.

8. Set the rack of lamb on a plate or disposable aluminum pan. Pour the Worcestershire sauce over the lamb along with 1 to 2 tablespoons of the butter mixture. Loosely cover with foil and let rest for 10 to 15 minutes.

9. Slice the rack of lamb between the bones. Fan the slices out on a serving platter and spoon the juices from the resting plate over the slices. Serve and take first place in your own home!

PRO TIP: Look for a rack that has been frenched, or has exposed bones with the meat removed between them. This makes for a great presentation and clean look.

For a clean presentation, wrap small strips of aluminum foil on each exposed bone before cooking. This will prevent the bones from charring and becoming brittle. It takes some time but is well worth it, in my opinion, because you eat with your eyes first.

HONEY TERIYAKI KALBI BEEF SHORT RIBS

SERVES 4 TO 6 / **PREP TIME:** 10 minutes, plus 4 to 6 hours marinating time
COOK TIME: 5 to 10 minutes / **SUGGESTED WOOD:** Applewood chips

This recipe takes me back to my US Navy days, when I was stationed in Pearl Harbor, Hawaii. There was a little Hawaiian barbecue hut we would visit, and the kalbi beef short ribs were the best in the world. The sweet sauce and the charred beef fat on these ribs will have you wishing you made more. Serve these with Hawaiian Mac Salad (page 170) and some sticky white rice for an authentic Hawaiian barbecue lunch plate. Flanken-cut short ribs are a cross-section cut from the beef plate ribs and sliced about ½ inch thick.

10 to 12 flanken-cut beef short ribs (2½ to 3 pounds)

1½ cups Sticky Honey Teriyaki Sauce (page 198), chilled and divided

2 cups cooked white rice, for serving

¼ cup sliced scallions

Toasted sesame seeds, for garnish

1. Place the ribs in a large resealable plastic bag. Pour three-quarters of the chilled teriyaki sauce in the bag and toss to coat all the ribs. Refrigerate for 4 to 6 hours.

2. Remove the ribs from the bag, place them on a plate, and discard the marinade. Use a paper towel to pat the ribs dry.

3. Set up your grill for direct cooking (see page 3). Fill a charcoal chimney with charcoal and light it with a fire starter cube. When the coals have turned gray, dump them into the grill grate or basket in an even layer, close the lid, and open the top and bottom vents. Right before you plan to cook, scatter a small handful of applewood chips directly on the hot coals.

4. Place the ribs evenly on the grate, close the lid, and cook for 1 to 2 minutes, then open the lid, rotate the ribs 90 degrees, close the lid, and cook for 1 to 2 minutes more. Open the lid and rotate the ribs again. If you're using a charcoal grill, keep the lid off to create a hot fire. Cook for another 1 to 2 minutes, rotating the ribs until they are nicely caramelized. The ribs are thin, so they will cook quickly.

5. Remove the ribs from the grill, lightly cover with foil, and let rest for 5 to 10 minutes.

6. To serve, place the ribs on a bed of sticky white rice, drizzle with the remaining teriyaki sauce, and top with sliced scallions and sesame seeds.

> **PRO TIP:** During the last few minutes of cooking, brush the ribs with some of the remaining sauce to create a nice char and crust on the outside. In my opinion, the crispy end tips are the best part.

LAMB SHOULDER BARBACOA

SERVES 6 TO 10 / **PREP TIME:** 30 to 45 minutes / **COOK TIME:** 6 to 7½ hours
SUGGESTED WOOD: Pecan wood chunks

I featured this recipe in one of my cooking videos and it quickly became a fan favorite. The lamb shoulder works so well in this recipe; the rich fat is caramelized from the high heat, creating an amazing texture and flavor.

1 (5- to 6-pound) lamb
    shoulder, bone in or out
4 to 5 tablespoons
    Southwestern
    Seasoning (page 197)
1 cup beef stock
2 whole chipotle chiles in
    adobo sauce, diced
4 garlic cloves,
    roughly chopped
1 white onion, diced
6 to 10 corn tortillas
1 avocado, pitted
    and peeled
2 limes
1 bunch cilantro, chopped
½ cup queso fresco,
    for serving
½ cup Mexican crema,
    for serving

1. Remove the excess fat from the lamb shoulder and season all sides with the seasoning mix. Set aside.

2. Set up your grill for indirect cooking (see page 4) and a long cook by filling the indirect side of the grill halfway with unlit coals. Fill a charcoal chimney with lump charcoal and light it with a fire starter cube. When the coals have turned gray, dump them into the grill on the side opposite the disposable aluminum pan so they are partially covering the unlit coals. Close the lid and open the top and bottom vents until the grill temperature registers about 275°F. Continue to monitor the grill, adjusting the vents as needed, until it reaches a cooking temperature of 300°F to 325°F. About 15 minutes before you plan to cook, place 2 or 3 medium pecan wood chunks directly on the hot coals, then close the lid.

3. Place the lamb shoulder on the indirect side of the grill directly over the drip pan and cook for 3 hours, rotating the shoulder halfway through. You are looking for the bark (crust) to be set and not flaking or wet.

4. Remove the shoulder from the grill and place it in a disposable aluminum half pan. In a small bowl, combine the beef stock and diced chipotle chiles and pour this mixture over the shoulder in the pan. Add the garlic and three-quarters of the onion to the pan, cover with aluminum foil, and return it to the indirect side of the grill. If you need to add fuel to the grill, do so while the lamb is foiled in the pan.

5. Cook for another 2 to 3 hours, until the lamb shoulder reaches an internal temperature of about 206°F. Use the probe of your thermometer to test the texture; you are looking for the probe to slide into the meat with little to no resistance.

6. When the lamb is properly tender, remove the pan from the grill and uncover the lamb. Pour the pan juices into a fat separator and set aside. Rest the shoulder for 15 minutes, then, using two forks, shred the lamb shoulder, garlic, and onion pieces all together and return it to the disposable pan. Add ½ cup of the reserved pan juices to the pulled lamb and toss to coat.

7. Place the pan, uncovered, back on the indirect side of the grill and cook for another 1 to 1½ hours, turning the meat every 20 minutes to caramelize the exterior. If the meat is looking too dry, add a couple of spoonfuls of the reserved pan juices to the lamb and toss to coat. When done, remove and let rest for 10 minutes while you prepare the toppings and tortillas.

8. Place the tortillas on the direct-heat side of the grill. Cook for 1 to 2 minutes, flip, and repeat, then set aside.

9. Smash the avocado to a chunky consistency, then season with a pinch of the seasoning and the juice of half a lime and stir well.

10. Add the chopped cilantro to the remaining one-quarter of the diced onion. Cut the remaining 1½ limes into wedges for serving.

11. To serve, fill a tortilla with pulled lamb meat, and top with avocado, the cilantro-onion mixture, queso fresco, and a drizzle of crema.

PRO TIP: If you like your barbacoa crispier, continue to cook it uncovered a bit longer. The fat will start to caramelize and create a nice crispy texture.

RIB-EYE STEAKS WITH GORGONZOLA CREAM SAUCE

SERVES 4 / PREP TIME: 30 to 45 minutes / **COOK TIME:** 8 to 10 minutes
SUGGESTED WOOD: Hickory wood chips

To be the king of the backyard barbecue, you must know how to cook an amazing steak. You'll be wearing the crown in no time with this recipe! I have also used a New York strip and filet for this recipe. Cook them the same way as you would a rib eye.

4 (1¼- to 1½-inch-thick) boneless rib-eye steaks

2 tablespoons SPGJ Rub (page 194)

1 teaspoon salted butter

2 garlic cloves, minced

1¼ cups heavy cream

1 tablespoon grated Parmesan cheese

¼ cup crumbled Gorgonzola cheese

½ teaspoon freshly ground black pepper

Avocado oil spray

2 tablespoons chopped Italian parsley

1. Trim the excess fat from each steak and season both sides with the rub, then set aside.

2. To make the cream sauce, melt the butter in a small saucepan or skillet over medium heat. Add the garlic and cook for 1 to 2 minutes. When the garlic is fragrant, add the heavy cream and heat to a slow boil, stirring constantly. You want the liquid in the cream to evaporate and reduce by about one-third. After it has reduced, remove the pan from the heat and add the Parmesan, Gorgonzola, and pepper. Stir to combine and set aside.

3. Set up your grill for direct cooking (see page 3). Fill a charcoal chimney with charcoal and light it with a fire starter cube. When the coals have turned gray, dump them into the grill grate or basket in an even layer, close the lid, and open the top and bottom vents. Right before you plan to cook, scatter a small handful of hickory wood chips directly on the hot coals, then close the lid

4. Spray the steaks with avocado oil on both sides and lay them on the grill. Close the lid and cook for 1½ to 2 minutes. Open the lid, rotate the steaks 90 degrees, close the lid, and cook for another 1½ to 2 minutes.

5. Open the lid and flip the steaks, then close the lid and cook for 1½ to 2 minutes. Open the lid and rotate the steaks 90 degrees. At this time, insert a probe into the center of fattest part of the steak. It should have an internal temperature of 135°F to 138°F, depending on how you like your steak cooked.

6. When the steaks are at your desired doneness, remove them from the grill, lightly cover them with aluminum foil, and let rest for 10 minutes. If needed, reheat the Gorgonzola cream sauce until warmed through.

7. Slice the steaks into strips and place them on a serving plate. Spoon the sauce over the slices, top with Italian parsley, and eat like a king!

PRO TIP: After seasoning them, I like to let my steaks come to room temperature for several hours before cooking. This allows the salt in the rub to interact with the meat proteins faster, resulting in a shorter cooking time and a more tender, juicier product.

BACKYARD BEEF BRISKET

SERVES 6 TO 8 / **PREP TIME:** 30 to 45 minutes / **COOK TIME:** 10 to 11 hours
SUGGESTED WOOD: Pecan wood chunks

Brisket is considered by some to be the king of meats. You can tell when brisket is done by the "feel" of the meat and not just the internal temperature. When you insert the probe end of your instant-read thermometer, the meat should feel like a stick of butter at room temperature.

1 (10- to 12-pound) whole
  packer brisket, point
  and flat
1 cup SPGJ Rub (page 194)
1 cup beef stock
6 to 8 slices white bread,
  for serving
Sliced pickles, for serving
Sliced jalapeños,
  for serving
1 white onion, sliced thin,
  for serving
Southwest Sweet Heat
  BBQ Sauce (page 199),
  for serving

1. Pat the brisket dry with a paper towel. Remove any excess fat or hanging pieces, making sure to expose the meat on the top side and leave a fat cap on the bottom about ¼ inch thick. Season all sides with the rub. You can season the brisket up to 8 hours before cooking, cover and let it rest in the refrigerator, then set it out at room temperature an hour before grilling.

2. Set up your grill for indirect cooking (see page 4) by filling the indirect side halfway with unlit coals. Fill a charcoal chimney with lump charcoal and light it with a fire starter cube. When the coals have turned gray, dump them into the grill on the side opposite the disposable aluminum pan so they are partially covering the unlit coals. Close the lid and open the top and bottom vents until the grill temperature registers about 275°F. Continue to monitor the grill, adjusting the vents as needed, until it reaches a temperature of 300°F to 325°F. About 15 minutes before you plan to cook, place 3 or 4 medium pecan wood chunks directly on the hot coals, then close the lid.

3. Place the brisket fat-side down over the drip pan on the indirect side and close the lid. Monitor the temperature and cook for 2 ½ hours. Flip the brisket over so it is fat-side up, then replace the lid. Cook for 2 ½ hours more and check the bark (crust) on the brisket. The seasoning should be set into the meat and not wet or crumbly.

4. On a table, arrange two long sheets of heavy-duty aluminum foil, twice the length of the brisket, crossing one over the other in the middle like a plus sign. After 5 hours, or when the bark is set, remove the brisket from the grill and lay it fat-side down on the foil. Shape the foil around the brisket like a boat. Pour the beef stock around the brisket and seal each end of the foil tightly around the brisket. This is a good time to check the grill and add more fuel if needed.

5. Place the foil-wrapped brisket back on the indirect side of the grill and cook for another 3 hours. Open the lid, rotate the brisket 180 degrees, and close the lid. Cook for another hour, then test for tenderness and get an internal temperature reading. Using an instant-read thermometer, take the readings from the top in two places, making sure not to poke a hole in the foil too low or the liquid will leak. You are looking for the probe to slide into the meat with little to no resistance and an internal temperature of 205°F to 208°F. This may take another 2 to 3 hours. Do not rush it; great barbecue takes time.

6. When the brisket is probing smoothly, remove it from the grill and open the foil to vent some of the heat for 5 to 10 minutes, then close the foil tightly and rest the brisket in an unlit oven for at least 1½ hours. Open the foil to release the steam and let the brisket rest on your counter at room temperature.

7. When ready to serve, remove the brisket from the foil and place it on a cutting board. Slice across the grain and cut the point muscle (the larger end) into cubes for "burnt ends." Use the drippings in the foil to keep the brisket slices moist after slicing.

8. Serve the brisket on a slice of white bread with pickles, jalapeños, sliced onions, and the barbecue sauce on the side.

PRO TIP: Not all briskets are equal. A lesser-grade brisket like Select or Choice will be done before a higher grade like Prime or Wagyu. More marbling in Prime and Wagyu breeds allows you to push your cook time a bit longer while maintaining the integrity and structure of the meat. Always look for a high-grade brisket or one with as much intramuscular fat or marbling as possible.

SMOKED MEATBALL SUB

SERVES 4 TO 6 / **PREP TIME:** 30 to 45 minutes / **COOK TIME:** 30 to 45 minutes
SUGGESTED WOOD: Applewood chunks

Meatballs are so easy to make, and cooking them on your grill gives them another level of flavor. These moist on the inside and smoky and crusty on the outside meatballs are the perfect filling for a sandwich. I have also made these meatballs with ground turkey and ground chicken.

**1 pound 80/20
  ground beef**

½ pound ground pork

**1 pound hot or sweet
  ground Italian sausage**

**½ cup dried
  bread crumbs**

2 large eggs, beaten

**¼ cup shredded
  Parmesan cheese**

**2 tablespoons Italian
  seasoning**

Salt

**Freshly ground
  black pepper**

4 to 6 sub or hoagie rolls

Avocado oil spray

**2 cups marinara or
  tomato sauce**

**8 to 10 slices
  provolone cheese**

**2 tablespoons chopped
  fresh basil**

1. In a large bowl, combine the ground beef, pork, and sausage. Add the bread crumbs, eggs, Parmesan, Italian seasoning, and salt and pepper to taste. Mix thoroughly. Using your hands, form 12 to 15 meatballs. Set aside.

2. Set up your grill for indirect cooking (see page 4). Fill a charcoal chimney with lump charcoal and light it with a fire starter cube. When the coals have turned gray, dump them into the grill on the side opposite the disposable aluminum pan, replace the cooking grate, close the lid, and open the top and bottom vents until the grill temperature registers about 275°F. Continue to monitor the grill, adjusting the vents as needed, until it reaches a cooking temperature of 300°F to 325°F. About 15 minutes before you plan to cook, add 1 or 2 medium applewood chunks directly on the hot coals, then close the lid.

3. When the grill is ready, open the lid and add the meatballs to the indirect side of the grill over the drip pan. Cook for 20 minutes, then rotate the meatballs and check the internal temperature with an instant-read thermometer. When the meatballs reach about 150°F, move them to the direct side to char.

4. Rotate the meatballs for 1 to 2 minutes on the direct side of the grill to get a crust on all sides. Cook until the meatballs reach an internal temperature of 160°F, then remove them from the grill and set aside.

5. Spray the sub rolls with avocado oil and place them on the grates directly over the fire for 1 to 2 minutes to toast.

6. To build a sandwich, place the bottom bun on a plate. Spoon a tablespoon of marinara sauce on the bottom bun; add 3 or 4 meatballs; top with more sauce, 2 slices of provolone cheese, and chopped basil; and finish with the top bun.

PARMESAN-CRUSTED LAMB CHOPS

SERVES 4 TO 6 / **PREP TIME:** 30 to 45 minutes / **COOK TIME:** 20 to 25 minutes
SUGGESTED WOOD: Pecan wood chunks

I picked up this recipe during my travels through Australia. Lamb is a local favorite Down Under and served everywhere. I love the flavors the grill gives the lamb while it still gets the crispy crust of a deep-fried chop. You will need to cook a little hotter to get a nice crispy crust on these chops.

10 to 12 bone-in lamb
   chops (2 to 2½ pounds)
2 teaspoons salt, divided
2 teaspoons freshly
   ground black
   pepper, divided
1 cup dried bread crumbs
¼ cup grated
   Parmesan cheese
1 teaspoon Italian
   seasoning
1 teaspoon paprika
1 teaspoon garlic powder
1 large egg, beaten
2 tablespoons water
½ cup all-purpose flour
Avocado oil spray

1. Trim the lamb chops of excess fat, sprinkle with 1 teaspoon each of salt and pepper, and set aside.

2. Set up your grill for indirect cooking (see page 4). Fill a charcoal chimney with lump charcoal and light it with a fire starter cube. When the coals have turned gray, dump them into the grill on the side opposite the disposable aluminum pan, replace the cooking grate, close the lid, and open the top and bottom vents until the grill temperature registers about 325°F. Continue to monitor the grill, adjusting the vents as needed, until it reaches a cooking temperature of 350°F to 375°F. About 15 minutes before you plan to cook, place 1 or 2 medium pecan wood chunks directly on the hot coals, then close the lid.

3. In a large resealable plastic bag, combine the bread crumbs, Parmesan, the remaining 1 teaspoon each salt and pepper, the Italian seasoning, paprika, and garlic powder. Shake well to blend.

4. In a bowl, mix together the beaten egg and water. Evenly spread the flour on a plate. Lightly coat a chop first in the flour, then the egg mixture, then the bread-crumb mixture. Pat the crumb mixture into the chop to make sure it is evenly coated, then set the chop aside. Repeat with the remaining chops, then spray one side of each chop with avocado oil.

5. Open the grill and lay the chops, oiled-side down, on the indirect side over the drip pan. Spray the top sides with avocado oil, replace the lid, and cook for 15 minutes. Open the lid, flip the chops, and test for doneness with an instant-read thermometer; you are looking for golden-brown chops with an internal temperature of 135°F to 138°F, which achieves a medium doneness (if you like your meat more well done, cook until the chops reach above 145°F). Close the lid and cook until the chops have reached your desired doneness. Remove them from the grill and let rest for 5 to 10 minutes before serving.

PRO TIP: Take these chops to another level with a drizzle of the chimichurri sauce from the leg of lamb recipe on page 68.

Skirt Steak Carne Asada Tacos with Avocado Crema

SERVES 4 TO 6 / **PREP TIME:** Up to 8 hours / **COOK TIME:** 10 to 20 minutes
SUGGESTED WOOD: Mesquite lump charcoal

Living in the Southwest, we eat Mexican food almost daily, and carne asada tacos are our go-to. The citrusy marinade and Southwestern flavors make this skirt steak tender and juicy. When charred over mesquite charcoal, they are hard to beat on Taco Tuesday or any day of the week.

Carne and Pollo Asada
Marinade (page 201)
1 (3- to 4-pound)
trimmed whole skirt
steak, cut into 4 or
5 equal-size pieces
2 large avocados, pitted
and peeled
Juice of 2 limes
½ bunch cilantro,
chopped, divided
¼ cup sour cream or
Mexican crema
½ teaspoon garlic powder
Salt
Freshly ground
black pepper
2 tablespoons
Southwestern
Seasoning (page 197)
6 to 8 scallions
1 tablespoon extra-virgin
olive oil
10 to 12 corn tortillas
1 small white onion, diced

1. Pour the marinade into a large resealable plastic bag. Place the pieces of skirt steak n the marinade and massage to coat all the pieces. Remove any air from the bag and place it in the refrigerator for up to 8 hours. Every hour or two, shift the meat in the bag to make sure all pieces are evenly coated.

2. In a blender or food processor, combine the avocados, lime juice, half the cilantro, the sour cream, garlic powder, and salt and pepper to taste and blend until the ingredients are thoroughly combined. Cover and refrigerate the avocado crema until you're ready to use.

3. When you're ready to cook, set up your grill for direct cooking (see page 4). Fill a charcoal chimney with mesquite lump charcoal and light it with a fire starter cube. When the coals have turned gray, dump them into the grill grate or basket in an even layer, close the lid, and open the top and bottom vents.

4. Remove the steak from the bag and discard the marinade. Pat the steak dry with paper towels and sprinkle it with a light coat of the seasoning. Place the scallions on a plate and drizzle them with the olive oil.

5. When the grill is ready, lift the lid and place the steak on the grill directly over the coals. Close the lid and cook for 2 to 3 minutes, then flip the steak, add the scallions to the grill, and cook for another 2 to 3 minutes (with the lid open if you're using a charcoal grill). Flip the scallions and remove them if too charred. When the steak caramelizes and reaches an internal temperature of about 135°F (or your desired doneness), remove it from the grill and let rest 5 to 10 minutes.

6. Grill the tortillas for 1 to 2 minutes, flip, and repeat. Remove them from the grill and set aside. In a small bowl, mix the diced white onion and the remaining cilantro. Cut the steak across the grain, then again with the grain to make ½-inch cubes.

7. To build your taco, take a tortilla, add some meat and top with avocado crema, the onion-cilantro mixture, and a squeeze of lime. *¡Salud!*

REVERSE-SEARED TRI-TIP CAPRESE SALAD ON GRILLED NAAN BREAD

SERVES 4 TO 6 / PREP TIME: 30 to 45 minutes / **COOK TIME:** 1 hour
SUGGESTED WOOD: Pecan wood chunks

Tri-tip is so versatile and can work in many recipes. We like to make this and use it in the center of a charcuterie board, surrounded with cheeses, olives, roasted red peppers, marinated mushrooms, and other items.

1 (2-pound) whole
   tri-tip roast
1½ tablespoons SPGJ Rub
   (page 194)
2 tablespoons
   Worcestershire sauce
2 tablespoons salted
   butter, melted
1 or 2 pieces naan bread
2 tablespoons extra-virgin
   olive oil, divided
3 or 4 Roma tomatoes
1 (8-ounce) ball fresh
   mozzarella cheese
10 to 12 fresh basil leaves
2 tablespoons
   balsamic glaze

1. Trim any excess fat from the tri-tip, including the fat cap. Season all sides with the rub and set aside. Feel free to season the tri-tip up to an hour before cooking.

2. Set up your grill for indirect cooking (see page 4). Fill a charcoal chimney with lump charcoal and light it with a fire starter cube. When the coals have turned gray, dump them into the grill on the side opposite the disposable aluminum pan, replace the cooking grate, close the lid, and open the top and bottom vents until the grill temperature registers about 275°F. Continue to monitor the grill, adjusting the vents as needed, until it reaches a cooking temperature of 300°F to 325°F. About 15 minutes before plan to cook, place 1 or 2 medium pecan wood chunks directly on the hot coals, then close the lid.

3. When the grill is running clean, place the tri-tip on the indirect side over the drip pan and cook for 30 minutes. Flip and rotate the tri-tip and cook it for 20 minutes more, then test the internal temperature by inserting an instant-read thermometer into the thickest part of the tri-tip. I like mine to reach 125°F to 128°F.

4. Once the tri-tip reaches this temperature, fully open the bottom vents to feed the fire and increase the temperature. Give the grill about 5 minutes to come up to temperature, then place the tri-tip directly over the coals to sear the outside.

5. Give each side a minute or two to crust up. Remove the tri-tip when the internal temperature reaches 135°F to 138°F, or your desired doneness. Place the tri-tip on a plate and pour the Worcestershire sauce and butter on top, lightly cover it with foil, and let rest for 10 to 15 minutes.

6. While the tri-tip is resting, brush the naan bread with 1 tablespoon of olive oil and place it on the grill directly over the coals. Cook for 1 to 2 minutes, then flip and cook for 1 to 2 minutes more, making sure it doesn't burn. Remove and set aside.

7. Slice the tomatoes and mozzarella. Cut the naan into 4 to 6 equal slices.

8. Place the tri-tip on a cutting board and thinly slice it across the grain. Place the slices back into the juices on the plate. Set a couple of slices of tri-tip on a piece of naan and top with tomato slices, mozzarella, and a basil leaf. Repeat with the remaining ingredients, then drizzle each portion with the remaining 1 tablespoon of olive oil and the balsamic reduction.

PRO TIP: Make sure to buy a highly marbled tri-tip. This will lead to a better product and juicier, more flavorful meat. I like to get a Prime grade or even a Wagyu for this cut.

THE ULTIMATE LAMB BURGER

SERVES 4 TO 6 / PREP TIME: 30 to 45 minutes / **COOK TIME:** 10 to 15 minutes
SUGGESTED WOOD: Oak wood chips

This recipe is inspired by my great friend Dan Barrett from Big Smoke BBQ out of Melbourne, Australia. We shot a recipe video at the 2019 American Royal World Series of Barbecue and featured a lamb shoulder gyro. He made a tzatziki sauce that paired perfectly with the lamb.

2 pounds ground lamb

1½ tablespoons SPGJ Rub (page 194)

½ cup crumbled feta cheese

1 recipe Homemade Tzatziki Sauce (page 191)

4 to 6 hamburger buns

1 head iceberg lettuce, shredded

1 white onion, thinly sliced

3 Roma tomatoes, thinly sliced

1. Form the lamb into 4 to 6 equal-size patties. Season both sides with the rub and set aside.

2. Set up your grill for direct cooking (see page 3). Fill a charcoal chimney with charcoal and light it with a fire starter cube. When the coals have turned gray, dump them into the grill grate or basket in an even layer, close the lid, and open the top and bottom vents. Right before you plan to cook, scatter a small handful of oak wood chips directly on the hot coals.

3. When the grill is hot and the fire is running clean, place the lamb patties evenly around the grill, close the lid, and cook for 1 to 2 minutes. Rotate the burgers 90 degrees, replace the lid, and cook for another 1 to 2 minutes. Open the lid and flip the burgers, then replace the lid. Cook for 1 to 2 minutes, then rotate the burgers 90 degrees. At this point, check the internal temperature; for ground lamb the USDA recommends 160°F. When near your preferred doneness, flip the burgers again and top each patty with some feta cheese. Close the lid and cook for 1 minute, or until the cheese melts slightly. Remove the burger patties, cover lightly with foil, and let rest for 5 to 10 minutes.

4. To serve, place a spoonful of tzatziki on the bottom bun, add a burger patty and another dollop of tzatziki, and top with shredded lettuce, onion slices, tomato slices, and more tzatziki. Cover with top bun and enjoy.

Citrus-Marinated Flank Steak

SERVES 4 TO 6 / PREP TIME: 6 hours to overnight / **COOK TIME:** 12 to 15 minutes
SUGGESTED WOOD: Applewood chips

This dish can be added to sandwiches, tacos, or pitas, or eaten just by itself. The citrus marinade breaks down the tight muscle fibers, turning this into a very tender and juicy steak.

Juice of 3 oranges
Juice of 3 lemons
Juice of 3 limes
6 garlic cloves, minced
¼ cup soy sauce
¼ cup olive oil
1 teaspoon salt
1 teaspoon freshly ground
  black pepper
1 whole (2-pound) flank
  steak, trimmed of
  excess fat
1½ tablespoons SPGJ Rub
  (page 194)

1. In a large resealable plastic bag, combine the orange, lemon, and lime juices with the garlic, soy sauce, olive oil, salt, and pepper. Place the flank steak in the bag to marinate in the refrigerator for 6 to 8 hours or overnight.

2. Remove the flank steak from the bag and discard the marinade. Pat the steak dry with paper towels and give it a light coating of the rub.

3. Set up your grill for direct cooking (see page 3). Fill a charcoal chimney with charcoal and light it with a fire starter cube. When the coals have turned gray, dump them into the grill grate or basket in an even layer, close the lid, and open the top and bottom vents. Right before you plan to cook, scatter a small handful of applewood chips on the hot coals.

4. When the grill is ready, lift the lid and place the flank steak directly over the coals. Close the lid and cook for 2 to 3 minutes. Lift the lid and rotate the flank steak 90 degrees. Close the lid and cook for 2 to 3 minutes more. Open the lid and flip the flank steak. Keeping the lid up for the last several minutes if you're using a charcoal grill, cook for another 2 to 3 minutes, then rotate the steak 90 degrees and continue cooking until your desired doneness is reached. For this cut, I like it to reach an internal temperature of 135°F to 138°F.

5. Remove it from the grill, cover lightly with foil, and let rest for 10 to 15 minutes. Place the flank steak on a cutting board and slice across the grain. Serve and enjoy!

Gyro Skewers with Chopped Mediterranean Salad

SERVES 4 TO 6 / **PREP TIME:** 45 minutes, plus 1- to 2-hour rest / **COOK TIME:** 10 to 15 minutes / **SUGGESTED WOOD:** Pecan wood chips

I have grown very fond of lamb, thanks to my many travels to Australia. These skewers can be served with the chopped salad in this recipe, or try them on a warm pita with lettuce, tomato, onion, feta cheese, and tzatziki sauce (see page 191 for my homemade version).

1 pound ground lamb

½ pound 80/20 ground beef

2 or 3 garlic cloves, finely diced

2 tablespoons diced scallions

1 tablespoon chopped fresh marjoram leaves

1 tablespoon Italian seasoning

Salt

Freshly ground black pepper

1 head iceberg lettuce, diced

½ to 1 small white onion, chopped

1 cucumber, chopped

2 Roma tomatoes, diced

½ cup crumbled feta cheese

Grilled naan or pita bread, for serving

1. In a large bowl, combine the lamb, beef, garlic, scallions, marjoram, Italian seasoning, and salt and pepper to taste. Form the meat into 6 equal-size log shapes and insert a long wood or metal skewer lengthwise into each log through its middle. Cover and refrigerate the skewers for 1 to 2 hours.

2. Set up your grill for direct cooking (see page 3). Fill a charcoal chimney with charcoal and light it with a fire starter cube. When the coals have turned gray, dump them into the grill grate or basket in an even layer, close the lid, and open the top and bottom vents. When the grill temperature reaches 450°F, scatter a small handful of pecan wood chips on the hot coals.

3. Lift the lid and place the skewers directly over the coals. Close the lid and cook for 1 to 2 minutes. Lift the lid and roll the skewers a quarter turn, close the lid, and cook for 1 to 2 minutes more. Open the lid and give them another quarter turn. Keep the lid up for the last several minutes and cook for another 1 to 2 minutes, continuing to rotate the skewers until your desired doneness is reached. Per the USDA, ground lamb and beef need to reach an internal temperature of 160°F.

4. Remove the skewers from the grill to a platter and lightly cover them with foil. Let rest for 5 to 10 minutes.

5. While the skewers are resting, layer a bed of lettuce, chopped onion, chopped cucumber, and tomato on a plate. Lay the skewers on the salad and top with crumbled feta cheese. Serve with grilled bread and enjoy!

PRO TIP: Wrapping each skewer in plastic wrap before chilling will help keep the shape of the gyro skewers. Drizzle some Homemade Tzatziki Sauce (page 191) over these skewers and the salad to make it legendary!

VENISON BACKSTRAP WITH BACON-SAGE BUTTER

SERVES 4 TO 6 / **PREP TIME:** 8 hours / **COOK TIME:** 10 to 15 minutes
SUGGESTED WOOD: Cherrywood chips

I was picked to compete in a championship pitmaster throwdown several years ago with a mystery ingredient, which ended up being venison. This is the recipe I made, and the judges gave me the win that day. I like using cherrywood with venison, as its natural sweetness complements the meat nicely.

½ cup extra-virgin
   olive oil
¼ cup soy sauce
1 tablespoon apple
   cider vinegar
4 or 5 garlic cloves, diced
1 teaspoon onion powder
1 teaspoon red
   pepper flakes
2 (1½- to 2-pound)
   venison backstraps,
   trimmed of excess fat
1 cup (2 sticks) salted
   butter, softened
3 or 4 cooked bacon
   slices, crumbled, plus
   extra for garnish
6 to 8 dried sage leaves,
   crumbled, or fresh
   leaves cooked in bacon
   fat and chopped
2 tablespoons SPGJ Rub
   (page 194)

1. In a large resealable plastic bag, combine the olive oil, soy sauce, apple cider vinegar, garlic, onion powder, and red pepper flakes. Add the backstraps, seal the bag, and refrigerate for up to 8 hours.

2. In a small bowl, combine the butter, crumbled bacon, and sage leaves. Cover and refrigerate until ready to use.

3. Set up your grill for direct cooking (see page 3). Fill a charcoal chimney with charcoal and light it with a fire starter cube. When the coals have turned gray, dump them into the grill grate or basket in an even layer, close the lid, and open the top and bottom vents. Right before you plan to cook, scatter a small handful of cherrywood chips directly on the hot coals.

4. Remove the venison from the bag and discard the marinade. Pat the venison dry with paper towels, tie or truss if needed, and sprinkle it with a moderate coat of the rub.

5. When the grill is ready, lift the lid and place the venison directly over the coals. Close the lid and cook for 2 to 3 minutes. Lift the lid and rotate the backstraps 90 degrees. Close the lid and cook for 2 to 3 minutes more. Open the lid and flip the backstraps, then place a few dollops of the bacon-sage butter on the backstraps. Cook for an additional 2 to 3 minutes, keeping the lid up if you're using a charcoal grill, then rotate the meat 90 degrees, add a few more dollops of butter, and continue cooking until your desired doneness is reached. I like mine medium-rare, 135°F to 138°F.

6. Remove the venison from the grill, place a couple of spoonfuls of the bacon-sage butter on top, lightly cover it with foil, and let rest for 5 to 10 minutes.

7. Place the rested backstraps on a cutting board and slice them into medallions. Spoon the reserved butter from the plate over the medallions, top with extra bacon, and serve.

PRO TIP: Keep the internal temperature of the backstraps under 145°F. Backstrap is a very lean muscle and tends to dry out if it's cooked too long.

BONE-IN PRIME RIB WITH HERB BUTTER

SERVES 4 TO 6 / **PREP TIME:** 30 to 45 minutes / **COOK TIME:** 3 to 4 hours
SUGGESTED WOOD: Pecan wood chunks

This bone-in prime rib recipe is perfect for family gatherings around the holidays. If you cannot find a bone-in rib roast, you can use a boneless rib, but you may find that the cook time will be a little shorter. Have your butcher truss it for even cooking.

1 (5- to 6-pound) bone-in
   prime rib, trimmed of
   excess fat and trussed
Salt
Freshly ground
   black pepper
1 cup (2 sticks) salted
   butter, softened
1 tablespoon chopped
   fresh rosemary
1 tablespoon
   minced garlic
1 tablespoon
   onion powder
2 teaspoons red
   pepper flakes
2 to 3 cups beef stock, as
   needed, divided
1 large red onion, sliced

1. Lightly season the prime rib with salt and black pepper and set it aside at room temperature.

2. In a large bowl, combine the softened butter, rosemary, garlic, onion powder, 1 tablespoon each of salt and black pepper, the onion powder, and red pepper flakes. Set aside.

3. Set up your grill for indirect cooking (see page 4). Fill a charcoal chimney with lump charcoal and light it with a fire starter cube. When the coals have turned gray, dump them into the grill on the side opposite the disposable aluminum pan, replace the cooking grate, close the lid, and open the top and bottom vents until the grill temperature registers about 275°F. Continue to monitor the grill, adjusting the vents as needed, until it reaches a cooking temperature of 300°F to 325°F. About 15 minutes before you plan to cook, place 1 or 2 medium pecan wood chunks directly on the hot coals, then close the lid.

4. Slather the prime rib all over with the herb butter, concentrating on the meat side. Add 2 cups of beef stock and the sliced onion to the drip tray below the grill grates.

5. When the grill is hot and the fire is running clean, place the prime rib on the indirect side over the drip pan holding the beef stock and onion, close the lid, and cook for 1 hour. After 1 hour, rotate the prime rib 180 degrees and test the internal temperature. I like my prime rib around 135°F. At this point, if the drip pan is running low on liquid, you can add the remaining 1 cup of beef stock. Close the lid and cook until the prime rib reaches your desired doneness.

6. Remove the prime rib and the drip tray from the grill. Place the prime rib on a platter, cover lightly with aluminum foil, and let it rest for 20 to 30 minutes.

7. Place the prime rib on a cutting board, cut the twine, and remove and discard it. Slice in between the bones and place the slices on a serving tray. Spoon the stock-onion jus over the top and serve.

PRO TIP: Set the prime rib out at room temperature for 20 to 30 minutes before cooking so the butter does not harden and become difficult to work around the meat.

Beer and Onion Braised Beef Short Ribs

SERVES 4 TO 6 / **PREP TIME:** 30 to 45 minutes / **COOK TIME:** 3 to 3½ hours
SUGGESTED WOOD: Hickory wood chunks

These short ribs are tender, juicy, and full of flavor. They can be braised in a disposable aluminum pan or a cast-iron Dutch oven, which I prefer. The Dutch oven will contain and radiate the heat to help the ribs cook faster.

6 to 8 beef short ribs, individually cut and trimmed of excess fat
2 tablespoons SPGJ Rub (page 194)
2 cups beef stock
1 (12-ounce) can dark beer
2 sweet onions, sliced
4 or 5 garlic cloves, peeled
2 bay leaves
2 or 3 thyme sprigs
Pinch salt
Pinch freshly ground black pepper
¼ cup diced scallions

1. Season all sides of the short ribs with the rub and set aside.

2. Set up your grill for indirect cooking (see page 4). Fill a charcoal chimney with lump charcoal and light it with a fire starter cube. When the coals have turned gray, dump them into the grill on the side opposite the disposable aluminum pan, replace the cooking grate, close the lid, and open the top and bottom vents until the grill temperature registers about 275°F. Continue to monitor the grill, adjusting the vents as needed, until it reaches a cooking temperature of 300°F to 325°F. About 15 minutes before you plan to cook, place 1 or 2 medium hickory wood chunks directly on the hot coals, then close the lid.

3. Prepare the braising liquid by pouring the beef stock, beer, sliced onions, garlic, bay leaves, thyme, salt, and pepper in a disposable aluminum pan or Dutch oven with a lid.

4. When the grill is hot and the fire is running clean, place the short ribs on the indirect side over the drip pan, close the lid, and cook for 30 to 45 minutes. Lift the lid and rotate the short ribs 180 degrees. At this point, add the pan or Dutch oven with the braising liquid to the grill. You may notice the bones starting to poke out a bit from the ribs. Continue cooking another 30 to 45 minutes until the bark (crust) is set and the bones are poking out of one end.

5. Transfer the short ribs to the pan or Dutch oven and cover with foil or the lid. Return the pan to the grill and cook for another 1½ hours. Rotate the Dutch oven and test the meat with your instant-read thermometer. You are looking for the probe to slide into the meat with little to no resistance. If the ribs give resistance, replace the lid and cook for another 30 minutes before testing again.

6. When the ribs are probing smoothly, remove the Dutch oven from the grill to rest for 15 to 20 minutes. To plate, remove a rib from the pan and pour a couple of spoonfuls of the braising liquid over it, then top with diced scallions.

LEG OF LAMB WITH CHIMICHURRI SAUCE

SERVES 6 TO 8 / **PREP TIME:** 30 to 45 minutes / **COOK TIME:** 2 to 3 hours
SUGGESTED WOOD: Pecan wood chunks

I have hosted the main stage at several barbecue festivals across the country. This leg of lamb recipe is from my great friend Mike Johnson, owner of Sugarfire Smoke House. He made this leg of lamb with chimichurri sauce at one of the events, and I was instantly hooked. The natural lamb flavors meld perfectly with the fresh, tangy chimichurri sauce. There is also something to be said about cooking a whole leg of lamb on the grill—it adds another level of flavor.

1 (5- to 7-pound) leg of
   lamb, trimmed of excess
   fat and silver skin
19 garlic cloves,
   peeled, divided
1 cup plus
   2 to 3 tablespoons
   extra-virgin olive
   oil, divided
3 to 4 tablespoons SPGJ
   Rub (page 194)
1 bunch Italian parsley
Juice of 1 lemon
2 tablespoons red
   wine vinegar
1 teaspoon red
   pepper flakes
Pinch salt
Pinch freshly ground
   black pepper

1. Using a sharp knife, make twelve 2-inch-deep slits all over the leg of lamb and insert a garlic clove deep into each one.

2. Coat the leg with 2 to 3 tablespoons of olive oil, season it liberally with the rub, and set aside.

3. In a blender or food processor combine the parsley, lemon juice, red wine vinegar, red pepper flakes, salt, black pepper, and the remaining 7 garlic cloves. Pulse several times to break down the garlic and parsley, then drizzle in the remaining 1 cup of olive oil and process until well combined. Pour the chimichurri sauce into a bowl and set aside.

4. Set up your grill for indirect cooking (see page 4). Fill a charcoal chimney with lump charcoal and light it with a fire starter cube. When the coals have turned gray, dump them into the grill on the side opposite the disposable aluminum pan, replace the cooking grate, close the lid, and open the top and bottom vents until the grill temperature registers about 275°F. Continue to monitor the grill, adjusting the vents as needed, until

it reaches a cooking temperature of 300°F to 325°F. About 15 minutes before you plan to cook, place 1 or 2 medium pecan wood chunks directly on the hot coals, then close the lid.

5. When the grill is hot and the fire is running clean, place the leg of lamb on the indirect side over the drip pan, close the lid, and cook for 30 minutes. Rotate the leg of lamb 180 degrees, turn it over, and test the internal temperature. It should be 140°F to 145°F for medium-rare. Continue to cook and rotate every 30 minutes until your desired doneness is reached.

6. Remove the leg of lamb from the grill to a platter, cover lightly with aluminum foil, and let rest for 15 to 20 minutes.

7. Move the lamb to a cutting board and slice. Place the slices on a serving plate and top with chimichurri sauce.

PRO TIP: A leg of lamb is made up of several muscle groups. Try to remove as much exterior or intermuscular fat and silver skin as possible, which will help the seasoning adhere to the leg and allow the meat to absorb more smoke and flavor.

Chapter 4

PORK

◀ Southern Pulled Pork
Sandwich (page 88)

CHAMPIONSHIP PORK SPARERIBS

SERVES 4 TO 6 / **PREP TIME:** 1 hour / **COOK TIME:** 3 to 3½ hours
SUGGESTED WOOD: Pecan wood chunks

When I started in competition barbecue, spareribs was one of the first meats I wanted to perfect. There is nothing better than a perfectly cooked sweet and smoky pork rib. It's what barbecue dreams are made of. This recipe will win over your friends and family just as much as the competition judges.

1 (3½- to 4-pound) rack pork spareribs, trimmed St. Louis–style
2 teaspoons salt, divided
5 tablespoons Sweet and Savory Rub (page 195)
Butter-flavored vegetable oil spray
½ cup brown sugar, divided
8 tablespoons (1 stick) salted butter, sliced into 1-tablespoon pats, divided
½ cup honey, divided
¼ cup peach nectar
Southwest Sweet Heat BBQ Sauce (page 199), to taste

1. Prepare the ribs by trimming any excess fat and removing the membrane from the bone side. This is done by sliding a butter knife under the first or largest bone and prying up the membrane. When the membrane is released from the bones, grab the end with a paper towel, gently peel the membrane off the bone side, and discard. Sprinkle the bone side with 1 teaspoon of salt, then flip it over and season the meat side with the remaining 1 teaspoon of salt. Let sit for 15 to 20 minutes.

2. Season the bone side with the rub and let sit for 20 minutes. Flip and repeat on the meat side. Let the seasoning set in at room temperature for at least 30 minutes; you want the ribs to start "sweating" and look wet.

3. Set up your grill for indirect cooking (see page 4). Fill a charcoal chimney with lump charcoal and light it with a fire starter cube. When the coals have turned gray, dump them into the grill on the side opposite the disposable aluminum pan, replace the cooking grate, close the lid, and open the top and bottom vents until the grill temperature registers 275°F. Continue to monitor the grill, adjusting the vents as needed, until it reaches a cooking temperature of 300°F to 325°F. About 15 minutes before you plan to cook, place 1 or 2 medium pecan wood chunks directly on the hot coals, then close the lid.

4. When the grill reaches temperature, place the ribs bone-side down on the indirect side of the grill. Cook for 1 hour, then flip them and continue to cook for 1 hour more, or until the bark (or crust) is a deep mahogany color. If any pieces look dry, spray with butter.

5. Remove the ribs from the grill. On a counter or work surface, place two sheets of heavy-duty aluminum foil long enough to wrap the ribs completely. In a line down the middle of the foil, sprinkle half the brown sugar, half the pats of butter, and half the honey. Place the ribs bone-side down on the brown sugar mixture and repeat with the remaining brown sugar, butter, and honey on the other side of the ribs. Bring the long ends of the foil together and crimp to seal on top. On one end of the ribs, crimp the foil closed to seal, leaving the other end open. At the open end, pour the peach nectar into the foil, then crimp that end closed, making sure there are no holes or leaks. Wrap the foil tightly against the ribs so they braise in the ingredients.

6. Return the ribs to the indirect side of the grill, maintaining a grill temperature of 275°F to 300°F. Continue to cook for another 45 minutes to 1 hour, then test the ribs for doneness by opening the foil and inserting an instant-read thermometer. You are looking for the thermometer to slide into the meat between the bones with minimal to no resistance and an internal temperature of about 206°F. When done, remove the ribs from the grill and open the foil to vent and release some of the heat, then brush ¼ cup of barbecue sauce on the ribs. After 5 to 10 minutes, close the foil and let the ribs rest for 20 to 30 minutes.

7. To serve, remove the ribs from the foil packet and place on a cutting board, bone-side up. Brush with a light coat of barbecue sauce, then slice between the bones. Flip the ribs over and brush with more sauce, if desired.

PRO TIP: Before wrapping your ribs in foil, remove any excess caramelized pieces or crusty ends that might puncture the foil and let the braising liquid leak out. I also reserve some of the braising liquid to brush over the ribs after slicing to add more flavor and to keep the ends from drying out and oxidizing. These ribs are perfect served alone or alongside your favorite sides, like grilled corn on the cob.

Green Chile Pulled Pork Tacos

SERVES 6 TO 10 / **PREP TIME:** 30 minutes / **COOK TIME:** 4½ to 5 hours
SUGGESTED WOOD: Hickory wood chunks

This green chile pulled pork is full of flavor and can easily be used in other recipes. We have made enchiladas, pizzas, and even omelets with the leftovers. The Southwestern flavors in the seasoning and the green chiles pair well with the sweet, fatty pork.

1 (5- to 6-pound) pork shoulder, bone in or out, trimmed of excess fat

3 to 4 tablespoons Southwestern Seasoning (page 197)

1 cup roasted green chiles, peeled, seeded, and diced

4 garlic cloves, diced

½ cup chicken stock

10 soft flour tortillas

2 or 3 avocados, pitted, peeled, and sliced

1 small white onion, diced

1 bunch cilantro, chopped

1 cup crumbled cotija cheese

1. Season all sides of the pork shoulder with the seasoning and set aside. You can season the pork a few hours ahead of time and set it in the refrigerator; 30 minutes to an hour before you plan to grill, remove and let it set at room temperature.

2. Set up your grill for indirect cooking (see page 4). Fill a charcoal chimney with lump charcoal and light it with a fire starter cube. When the coals have turned gray, dump them into the grill on the side opposite the disposable aluminum pan, replace the cooking grate, close the lid, and open the top and bottom until the grill temperature registers about 275°F. Continue to monitor the grill, adjusting the vents as needed, until it reaches a cooking temperature of 300°F to 325°F. About 15 minutes before you plan to cook, place 1 or 2 medium hickory wood chunks directly on the hot coals, then close the lid.

3. When the grill is up to temperature and the smoke is clean, place the shoulder, fat-side down, on the indirect side of the grill over the drip pan. Close the lid and cook for 2 hours. Flip the pork shoulder and cook for another 1½ hours with the lid closed.

4. Transfer the shoulder from the grill to a disposable aluminum pan, fat-side down. Add the green chiles, garlic, and chicken stock. Tightly cover the pan with foil and place it on the indirect side, close the lid, and cook for 1 hour, then rotate the pan and test for tenderness. You are looking for very little to no resistance when the pork is probed and an internal temperature of 205°F to 208°F. If it needs more time, cook for another 30 minutes, rotate, and test again until it probes smoothly and cleanly.

5. Remove the pan from the grill and let rest for 20 to 30 minutes. Remove the foil and, using two forks, shred the pork right in the pan.

6. Warm the tortillas on the grill over the coals for a minute per side. To serve, place some pork on a warm tortilla and top with avocado slices, diced onion, cilantro, and some crumbled cotija cheese.

PRO TIP: For the best results, wait until the pork shoulder probes smoothly, like warm butter, before pulling it off the grill. This may take some extra time, but it's worth the wait for a tender product.

DOUBLE SMOKED HAM WITH BROWN SUGAR AND MAPLE GLAZE

SERVES 6 TO 10 / **PREP TIME:** 30 minutes / **COOK TIME:** 3 to 4 hours
SUGGESTED WOOD: Maple wood chunks

This recipe uses a store-bought precooked ham and is super easy. You can use a spiral-cut ham or not; I have made it both ways and found the spiral-cut ham cooks slightly faster. The double smoking process adds an extra layer of flavor to the ham, and the sweet glaze is a perfect match.

1 (5- to 6-pound)
  precooked ham, bone
  in or out
3 to 4 tablespoons
  Sweet and Savory Rub
  (page 195)
3 tablespoons
  salted butter
¾ cup packed light
  brown sugar
½ cup maple syrup
¼ cup pineapple juice
1 tablespoon soy sauce
¼ teaspoon
  cayenne pepper

1. Pat the ham dry with a paper towel. Score the surface in a crisscross pattern ¼ to ½ inch deep. Season the ham on all sides with the rub and set it aside.

2. Set up your grill for indirect cooking (see page 4). Fill a charcoal chimney with lump charcoal and light it with a fire starter cube. When the coals have turned gray, dump them into the grill on the side opposite the disposable aluminum pan, replace the cooking grate, close the lid, and open the top and bottom vents until the grill temperature registers about 275°F. Continue to monitor the grill, adjusting the vents as needed, until it reaches a cooking temperature of 300°F to 325°F. About 15 minutes before you plan to cook, place 1 or 2 medium maple wood chunks directly on the hot coals, then close the lid.

3. When the grill is up to temperature and the smoke is clean, place the ham on the indirect side of the grill over the drip pan. Close the lid and cook for 1 hour. Rotate the ham, then cook for another hour with the lid closed.

4. While the ham is smoking, make the glaze. In a sauce-pan over medium heat, melt the butter, then add the brown sugar, maple syrup, pineapple juice, soy sauce, and cayenne. Stir to combine and heat through, making sure not to boil or burn the glaze. When the glaze is fully blended, remove it from the heat and set aside. It will thicken upon standing.

5. After the ham has cooked for 2 hours, test the internal temperature with an instant-read thermometer. I like to start glazing the ham when the internal temperature is between 120°F and 125°F. When the ham reaches this temperature, rotate it again and spoon half the glaze all over the ham, starting at the top. Close the lid and cook for 30 minutes more. Open the lid and glaze the ham again with the remainder of the glaze. Cook until the internal temperature of the ham is between 130°F and 138°F.

6. Remove the ham from the grill and place it in a large dish, then lightly cover with aluminum foil and rest for 15 to 20 minutes.

7. To serve, slice the ham into ¼- to ½-inch-thick slices. Lay the slices on a plate and spoon any leftover juices from the resting dish over the ham.

Pork Tenderloin Pinwheels
à la Richard Fergola

SERVES 4 TO 6 / **PREP TIME:** 30 minutes / **COOK TIME:** 1 hour
SUGGESTED WOOD: Applewood chunks

My good friend Richard Fergola from Fergolicious BBQ out of Gardner, Kansas, cooked these for an appetizer class we taught together. I love the flavor the pork tenderloin picks up from the grill, and the apples are a great complement and add wonderful texture. These can be served as an appetizer or a main course.

1 (1- to 1½-pound) pork
   tenderloin
2 tablespoons Sweet and
   Savory Rub (page 195)
1 (12-ounce)
   package bacon
1 cup packed light
   brown sugar
1 Granny Smith apple,
   cored and sliced
   into wedges
Southwest Sweet Heat
   BBQ Sauce (page 199),
   to taste

1. Slice the tenderloin lengthwise in strips about ¼ inch thick. You can usually get about 5 or 6 strips from an average-size pork tenderloin. Lay the strips flat across a cutting board.

2. Sprinkle some of the rub on the tenderloin slices, then lay a slice of bacon on top of a tenderloin strip, followed by some brown sugar. Add an apple wedge to one end and roll the tenderloin strip into a pinwheel shape. Secure the end with a toothpick or skewer, then season the outside with more of the rub. Repeat until you have 5 or 6 pinwheels.

3. Set up your grill for indirect cooking (see page 4). Fill a charcoal chimney with lump charcoal and light it with a fire starter cube. When the coals have turned gray, dump them into the grill on the side opposite the disposable aluminum pan, replace the cooking grate, close the lid, and open the top and bottom vents until the grill temperature registers about 250°F. Continue to monitor the grill, adjusting the vents as needed, until it reaches a cooking temperature 275°F to 300°F. About 15 minutes before you plan to cook, place 1 or 2 medium applewood chunks directly on the hot coals, then close the lid.

4. When the grill is up to temperature and the smoke is clean, place the pinwheels on the indirect side of the grill over the drip tray and cook for 30 minutes. Open the lid and flip the pinwheels, then replace the lid and cook for another 30 minutes.

5. Open the lid and check the internal temperature of the pork tenderloin; it should be 140°F to 145°F and the bacon should be cooked through.

6. Remove the pinwheels from the grill, dunk them into the barbecue sauce, and let rest for 5 to 10 minutes.

7. After resting, remove the toothpicks, slice the pinwheels in half, and serve with extra barbecue sauce on the side, if desired.

STICKY HONEY TERIYAKI BABY BACK RIBS

SERVES 4 TO 6 / **PREP TIME:** 30 minutes / **COOK TIME:** 3 to 3½ hours
SUGGESTED WOOD: Maple wood chunks

These sticky honey baby back ribs melt in your mouth and are fall-off-the-bone tender. I like to use baby or loin back ribs for this recipe. They are a little smaller and leaner than spareribs and are very flavorful. As with other rib cuts, look for great marbling and an evenly thick rack.

1 (2½-pound) rack pork baby back or loin back ribs

2 teaspoons SPGJ Rub (page 194)

¼ cup packed light brown sugar

¼ cup pineapple juice

2 teaspoons soy sauce

1½ cups Sticky Honey Teriyaki Sauce (page 198)

1 teaspoon toasted sesame seeds

¼ cup sliced scallions

1. Trim any excess fat from the ribs. Remove the membrane on the bone side of the ribs by sliding a butter knife under the membrane on the smallest bone and prying up to release it from the bone. After it is released, grab it with a paper towel and pull the membrane down, releasing it from the bone side of the ribs. Discard after removing.

2. Sprinkle the rub on the bone side of the ribs, then flip them over and season the meat side. Let the seasoning set on the ribs for 30 to 45 minutes at room temperature.

3. Set up your grill for indirect cooking (see page 4). Fill a charcoal chimney with lump charcoal and light it with a fire starter cube. When the coals have turned gray, dump them into the grill on the side opposite the disposable aluminum pan, replace the cooking grate, close the lid, and open the top and bottom vents until the grill temperature registers about 275°F. Continue to monitor the grill, adjusting the vents as needed, until it reaches a cooking temperature of 300°F to 325°F. About 15 minutes before you plan to cook, place 1 or 2 medium maple wood chunks directly on the hot coals, then close the lid.

4. When the grill is up to temperature and the smoke is clean, place the ribs bone-side down on the indirect side of the grill over the drip tray and cook for 1 hour. Open the lid and flip the ribs so they are now bone-side up. Close the lid and cook for another hour.

5. Transfer the ribs meat-side up onto two long heavy-duty sheets of aluminum foil. Add the brown sugar, pineapple juice, and soy sauce on top of the ribs and wrap them tightly in the foil. Place them back on the indirect side of the grill and cook for 30 minutes, then test for doneness by sliding an instant-read thermometer between the bones. You are looking for the ribs to probe smoothly with little to no resistance and an internal temperature of 203°F to 206°F. If the ribs are not probing smoothly, close the lid and cook for 15 minutes, then test again.

6. Remove the ribs from the grill. Open the foil packet and crimp it down on the sides to create a foil "boat" that the ribs sit in. Brush the meat side of the ribs with the teriyaki sauce and return them to the indirect side of the grill. Close the lid and cook for 15 to 20 minutes, until the sauce is set into the ribs.

7. Remove the ribs from the grill and let rest for 15 to 20 minutes, then place the ribs on a cutting board, meat-side down, and brush the bone side with more teriyaki sauce. Cut the ribs between the bones and place them on a serving platter. Sprinkle with sesame seeds and sliced scallions and serve with warm teriyaki sauce on the side.

HERB-CRUSTED PORCHETTA

SERVES 4 TO 6 / **PREP TIME:** 30 minutes / **COOK TIME:** 2 to 2½ hours
SUGGESTED WOOD: Pecan wood chunks

The rotisserie option, if available on your grill, is my preferred way to cook this porchetta. As it rotates, it self-bastes, creating a nice crispy exterior. If your grill doesn't have this option, no worries—it can be done on the grill grate just as easily.

1 (4- to 5-pound) pork belly, skin removed

2 teaspoons salt, divided

½ cup olive oil

3 or 4 garlic cloves, diced

2 tablespoons chopped fresh sage

2 tablespoons chopped fresh rosemary

2 teaspoons chopped fresh thyme

Juice of 1 lemon

1 teaspoon freshly ground black pepper

½ teaspoon red pepper flakes

1. Score both sides of the pork belly in a crisscross pattern about ¼ inch deep. Pat dry with a paper towel, sprinkle both sides with 1 teaspoon of salt, and set aside.

2. In a large mixing bowl, combine the olive oil, garlic, sage, rosemary, thyme, lemon juice, black pepper, red pepper flakes, and the remaining 1 teaspoon of salt.

3. Lay the pork belly on a flat surface and spread half the olive oil–herb mixture on the inside, or meat side, of the belly in an even layer. Roll the belly up into a cylindrical shape and truss it with lengths of butcher's twine 1 to 1½ inches apart. Spread the remainder of the olive oil–herb mixture over the outside of the pork belly and set aside.

4. Set up your grill for indirect cooking (see page 4). Fill a charcoal chimney with lump charcoal and light it with a fire starter cube. When the coals have turned gray, dump them into the grill on the side opposite the disposable aluminum pan, replace the cooking grate, close the lid, and open the top and bottom vents until the grill temperature registers about 275°F. Continue to monitor the grill, adjusting the vents as needed, until it reaches a cooking temperature of 300°F to 325°F. About 15 minutes before you plan to cook, place 1 or 2 medium pecan wood chunks directly on the hot coals, then close the lid.

5. When the grill is up to temperature, place the pork belly on the indirect side of the grill over the drip tray and cook for 1 hour. Open the lid and rotate the pork belly 180 degrees. Close the lid and cook for another hour.

6. After 2 hours, test the internal temperature of the pork belly with an instant-read thermometer. You are looking for an internal temperature of 180°F to 190°F. Continue to cook and rotate until it reaches that temperature.

7. When the pork belly reaches your desired doneness, transfer it from the grill to a plate and let rest uncovered for 15 to 20 minutes.

8. After resting, place the porchetta on a cutting board and remove and discard the butcher's twine. Slice the porchetta into 1-inch-thick slices and serve.

PRO TIP: The chimichurri sauce from the leg of lamb recipe on page 68 works amazingly with this recipe. After slicing and laying the porchetta on a serving platter, drizzle the chimichurri sauce over the slices. The fatty porchetta and the tangy, fresh chimichurri sauce are a great combination of flavors.

BONE-IN RACK OF PORK WITH SAGE BROWN BUTTER

SERVES 4 TO 6 / PREP TIME: 30 minutes / **COOK TIME:** 2 to 2½ hours
SUGGESTED WOOD: Applewood chunks

This recipe calls for a whole bone-in rack of pork. Depending on how many people you are serving, you can have a butcher cut the whole rack down into however many portions or bones you need. I look for a nice even rack with as much marbling as possible. Pork is much like beef in that more intramuscular fat will lead to a juicier, more tender finished product.

1 (5- to 6-pound) rack of pork, bone in

4 tablespoons SPGJ Rub (page 194)

8 tablespoons (1 stick) salted butter

3 garlic cloves, diced

10 to 12 fresh sage leaves

1. Trim any excess fat around the loin to expose the meat. Season it liberally with the rub and set aside at room temperature. Feel free to season the rack up to an hour before cooking.

2. In a medium saucepan, melt the butter over medium heat. When the butter starts to get frothy, add the garlic and sage leaves. Reduce the heat to medium-low, being sure not to let the butter boil. Cook the garlic and sage in the butter until the sage starts to get dry, 5 to 10 minutes. When the sage leaves start to crumble, remove them from the butter and set aside. Remove the butter from the heat as well and set aside.

3. Set up your grill for indirect cooking (see page 4). Fill a charcoal chimney with lump charcoal and light it with a fire starter cube. When the coals have turned gray, dump them into the grill on the side opposite the disposable aluminum pan, replace the cooking grate, close the lid, and open the top and bottom vents until the grill temperature registers about 275°F. Continue to monitor the grill, adjusting the vents as needed, until it reaches a cooking temperature of 300°F to 325°F. About

15 minutes before you plan to cook, place 1 or 2 medium applewood chunks directly on the hot coals, then close the lid.

4. When the grill is up to temperature, place the rack of pork on the indirect side of the grill over the drip tray and cook for 1 hour. Open the lid and rotate the rack 180 degrees. Close the lid and cook for another hour.

5. After 2 hours of cooking, test the internal temperature of the pork with an instant-read thermometer. You are looking for 140°F to 145°F.

6. When the rack of pork reaches the desired temperature, transfer it from the grill to a plate. Drizzle half the garlic butter over the rack and let it rest for 20 to 30 minutes, covered lightly with aluminum foil.

7. After resting, place the rack of pork on a cutting board and slice it between the bones. Place the slices on a serving tray and drizzle with any leftover liquid from the resting plate and the remaining garlic butter. Top the slices with the fried sage leaves and serve.

Pork Sausage Breakfast Fatty

SERVES 4 TO 6 / PREP TIME: 30 minutes / **COOK TIME:** 1 to 1½ hours
SUGGESTED WOOD: Maple wood chunks

What is a breakfast fatty, you ask? Well, it's an amazing combination of ground sausage or beef and any filling your heart desires. I love making these for breakfast and incorporating scrambled eggs, shredded cheese, and bacon. Try this fatty with mozzarella, sun-dried tomatoes, and basil for another twist.

3 pounds ground
   breakfast sausage
1 recipe Sweet and Savory
   Rub (page 195), divided
½ cup shredded sharp
   cheddar cheese, divided
3 eggs, scrambled
   and cooled
4 or 5 cooked bacon
   slices, crumbled
3 teaspoons chopped
   fresh chives, divided

1. On a large cutting board, lay a long strip of plastic wrap to fully cover the board. Spread the sausage in an even layer measuring 10 by 10 inches on the plastic wrap. Sprinkle it all over with half the rub. In the middle of the square, layer ¼ cup of shredded cheese, then the scrambled eggs, crumbled bacon, the remaining ¼ cup of cheese, and finally 1½ teaspoons of chives.

2. Roll one side of the meat square over the filling into a loaf, making sure to seal the sides and ends. Season the outside with the remaining rub. Wrap the loaf in plastic wrap and refrigerate.

3. Set up your grill for indirect cooking (see page 4). Fill a charcoal chimney with lump charcoal and light it with a fire starter cube. When the coals have turned gray, dump them into the grill on the side opposite the disposable aluminum pan, replace the cooking grate, close the lid, and open the top and bottom vents until the grill temperature registers about 275°F. Continue to monitor the grill, adjusting the vents as needed, until it reaches a cooking temperature of 300°F to 325°F. About 15 minutes before you plan to cook, place 1 or 2 medium maple wood chunks directly on the hot coals, then close the lid.

4. When the grill is up to temperature, place the fatty on the indirect side of the grill over the drip tray and cook for 20 to 25 minutes. Open the lid and rotate the fatty 180 degrees. Close the lid and cook for another 20 to 25 minutes.

5. After 40 to 50 minutes of cooking, test the internal temperature of the sausage with an instant-read thermometer. You are looking for 157°F to 160°F.

6. Remove the fatty from the grill and let it rest on a plate for 10 to 15 minutes, covered loosely with aluminum foil.

7. After resting, place the fatty on a cutting board and cut it into 1-inch-wide slices. Top with the remaining 1½ teaspoons of chives and serve.

PRO TIP: To help hold the shape of the fatty, roll it in plastic wrap completely and place in the refrigerator for an hour before cooking.

SOUTHERN PULLED PORK SANDWICH

SERVES 6 TO 8 / **PREP TIME:** 30 minutes / **COOK TIME:** 5 to 6 hours
SUGGESTED WOOD: Pecan wood chunks

I love how the fatty, sweet pork and crisp, tangy slaw pair together on this sandwich—they're the perfect complements for each other. Placed on a soft potato bun, this is heaven on a plate.

For the slaw

1 small head green
   cabbage, thinly
   shredded

¼ cup diced red onion

¼ cup diced pickles

⅓ cup Dijon mustard

⅓ cup mayonnaise

¼ cup honey

2 teaspoons sugar

Salt

Freshly ground
   black pepper

For the pulled pork

1 (5- to 6-pound) pork
   shoulder or butt, bone
   in or out

6 to 8 tablespoons
   Sweet and Savory Rub
   (page 195)

1 cup apple juice

6 to 8 soft potato
   hamburger buns

1. **TO MAKE THE SLAW:** In a large mixing bowl, combine the cabbage, red onion, pickles, Dijon mustard, mayonnaise, honey, and sugar. Taste and season with salt and pepper to your liking. Cover the slaw and refrigerate until ready to serve.

2. **TO MAKE THE PULLED PORK:** Trim any excess fat from the pork shoulder, leaving the fat cap on the bottom. Pat dry with paper towels and season liberally with the rub. Set aside.

3. Set up your grill for indirect cooking (see page 4). Fill a charcoal chimney with lump charcoal and light it with a fire starter cube. When the coals have turned gray, dump them into the grill on the side opposite the disposable aluminum pan, replace the cooking grate, close the lid, and open the top and bottom vents until the grill temperature registers about 275°F. Continue to monitor the grill, adjusting the vents as needed, until it reaches a cooking temperature of 300°F to 325°F. About 15 minutes before cooking, place 1 or 2 pecan wood chunks directly on the hot coals, then close the lid.

4. When the grill is up to temperature, place the shoulder fat-side down on the indirect side of the grill over the drip pan, close the lid, and cook for 2 hours. Open the lid and flip the shoulder over so it is fat-side up. Close the lid and cook for another hour.

5. On the counter or work surface, position two sheets of aluminum foil about four times the length of the shoulder in a plus-sign shape. After 3 hours of cooking, remove the shoulder and place it in the center of the aluminum foil, fat-side down. Crimp the foil around the shoulder and pour the apple juice around it. Tightly wrap the foil around the shoulder and return it to the indirect side of the grill. Close the lid and cook for 1½ hours. Open the lid, rotate the shoulder 180 degrees, and test the texture by inserting an instant-read thermometer into a few different places on the shoulder. You are looking for the probe to slide into the meat with very minimal to no resistance and an internal temperature of 203°F to 206°F. If the texture is tough and hard to probe, replace the grill lid and cook for another 20 minutes, then test again.

6. When the shoulder is probing smoothly, remove it from the grill and let rest in a pan, still wrapped in the foil, for 30 minutes to 1 hour.

7. After resting, open the foil, remove the shoulder, and place it in the pan used for resting. Pour the juices from the foil over the shoulder and, using two forks, shred the pork into the juices. For added flavor, sprinkle some of the rub into the shredded pork and mix to combine.

8. To serve, place a heaping pile of pulled pork on each bottom bun and top with a large scoop of the slaw. Top with the other half of the bun and take a huge bite!

PRO TIP: With large cuts like pork shoulder and beef brisket, the "feel" is especially important. You are looking for the probe end of the thermometer to slide into the meat with minimal to no resistance, like soft butter that has been sitting at room temperature for a couple of hours. While resting the pork shoulder, place it in an empty cooler or an unlit oven and cover it with a towel.

Hawaiian Pork Kabobs with Sweet Maui Onion and Pineapple

SERVES 6 TO 8 / **PREP TIME:** 30 minutes / **COOK TIME:** 15 to 20 minutes
SUGGESTED WOOD: Applewood chips

These Hawaiian pork kabobs are so easy to make and perfect for a quick lunch or dinner. Feel free to change up the meat—we have made these with beef, chicken, and even lamb. If you can't find sweet Maui onions, a Vidalia onion will work, too.

1 (1- to 1½-pound) pork
    tenderloin
1 pineapple, peeled,
    cored, and cut into
    1½-inch cubes
1 sweet Maui onion, cut
    into eighths
4 or 5 jalapeños,
    quartered
2 tablespoons Sweet and
    Savory Rub (page 195)
Avocado oil spray
Sticky Honey Teriyaki
    Sauce (page 198),
    to taste
¼ cup chopped
    macadamia nuts

1. Trim any excess fat and silver skin from the pork tenderloin and pat it dry with a paper towel. Cut it into 1½-inch cubes.

2. Skewer a piece of the pork, a pineapple cube, a few pieces of onion, and a jalapeño quarter. Continue to add the ingredients in order until the skewer is full, then repeat with the remaining skewers and ingredients. Season the skewers with the rub and set aside.

3. Set up your grill for direct cooking (see page 3). Fill a charcoal chimney with charcoal and light it with a fire starter cube. When the coals have turned gray, dump them into the grill grate or basket in an even layer, replace the cooking grate, close the lid, and open the top and bottom vents. Right before you plan to cook, scatter a small handful of applewood chips directly on the hot coals.

4. When the grill reaches at least 450°F (this can take 20 to 30 minutes), spray the kabobs with avocado oil, then place them on the grill evenly around the cooking grate. Close the lid and cook for 3 to 4 minutes, then rotate the skewers a quarter turn. Close the lid and cook for another 3 to 4 minutes. Open the lid and rotate the skewers another quarter turn. Close the lid and cook for 3 to 4 minutes more. Open the lid, rotate the skewers another quarter turn, and, if you're using a charcoal grill, cook the last few minutes with the lid off. Test the pork for doneness by inserting an instant-read thermometer. When the pork is about 140°F, brush the skewers with teriyaki sauce and cook over direct heat until the pork reaches an internal temperature of 145°F.

5. Remove the skewers from the grill to a plate and let rest for 5 minutes. Before serving, top with chopped macadamia nuts.

PRO TIP: If you are using wooden skewers, soak them in water for 20 minutes before use so they don't burn during the cook. You can use metal skewers as well.

CHAR SIU PORK BELLY

SERVES 6 TO 8 / **PREP TIME:** 8 hours to overnight / **COOK TIME:** 2 to 2½ hours
SUGGESTED WOOD: Cherrywood chunks

This pork belly is sweet and savory, and it will melt in your mouth. The charred bits and crispy ends are my favorite part. For this recipe, I like the internal temperature of the belly to be 180°F to 190°F, followed by a 15- to 20-minute rest. It will lead to a nice rendered soft fat but still have structure and not fall apart.

1 (4- to 5-pound) pork
   belly, skin removed
½ cup soy sauce
⅓ cup hoisin sauce
⅓ cup honey
3 or 4 garlic
   cloves, minced
1½ teaspoons sriracha
1 teaspoon toasted
   sesame oil
1 teaspoon Chinese
   five-spice powder
1 teaspoon grated
   fresh ginger
¼ cup sliced scallions,
   for topping

1. Cut the pork belly into four equal-size pieces.

2. In a large bowl, combine the soy sauce, hoisin, honey, garlic, sriracha, sesame oil, five-spice powder, and ginger and mix thoroughly. Add the pork belly pieces and toss to coat evenly. Cover the bowl and refrigerate at least 8 hours or overnight.

3. Remove the pork belly and discard the marinade.

4. Set up your grill for indirect cooking (see page 4). Fill a charcoal chimney with lump charcoal and light it with a fire starter cube. When the coals have turned gray, dump them into the grill on the side opposite the disposable aluminum pan, replace the cooking grate, close the lid, and open the top and bottom vent until the grill temperature registers about 275°F. Continue to monitor the grill, adjusting the vents as needed, until it reaches a cooking temperature of 300°F to 325°F. About 15 minutes before you plan to cook, place 1 or 2 medium cherrywood chunks directly on the hot coals, then close the lid.

5. When the grill is up to temperature, place the pork belly pieces on the indirect side of the grill over the drip pan, close the lid, and cook for 1 hour.

6. Flip the pork belly pieces, close the lid, and cook for another hour. After 2 hours, test the internal temperature of the pork with an instant-read thermometer; it should be 180°F to 190°F.

7. When the pork belly is done, remove it from the grill to a plate and let rest, loosely covered with aluminum foil, for 15 to 20 minutes. When ready to eat, place the pork belly on a cutting board and cut it into ¼-inch-thick slices. Top with the scallions and serve.

PRO TIP: I like to move the pork belly pieces to the direct side directly over the coals for the last few minutes of cooking to give the outside a nice char. It only takes a couple of minutes on both sides; just make sure the exterior doesn't burn.

PORK TENDERLOIN FAJITAS

SERVES 4 TO 6 / **PREP TIME:** 30 minutes / **COOK TIME:** 10 to 12 minutes
SUGGESTED WOOD: Mesquite lump charcoal

Fajitas are traditionally made with beef or chicken. I like using pork tenderloin, however, and cooking it hot and fast over mesquite charcoal. This is another recipe you can use your GrillGrates for, if you have them. I have cooked these fajitas on both the flat-top side and the grill side, and I like both ways.

2 (1- to 1½-pound) pork
   tenderloins
2 tablespoons
   Southwestern
   Seasoning (page 197)
1 large white onion
1 large red bell pepper
1 large green bell pepper
Avocado oil spray
8 to 12 flour tortillas
1 cup Mexican crema
1 cup crumbled
   queso fresco

1. Cut the tenderloins into strips about 3 inches long and ½ inch wide. Season all sides with the seasoning and set aside.

2. Cut the onion into large disks ¼ inch thick. Cut the bell peppers into quarters and remove the core and seeds.

3. Set up your grill for direct cooking (see page 3). Fill a charcoal chimney with mesquite lump charcoal and light it with a fire starter cube. When the coals have turned gray, dump them into the grill grate or basket in an even layer, replace the cooking grate, close the lid, and open the top and bottom vents. You are looking for a hot fire and a grill temperature at least 450°F.

4. When the grill is up to temperature, spray the onions and peppers with avocado oil and place them evenly around the grill. Spray the pork tenderloin pieces with avocado oil and place them on the grill as well. Close the lid and cook for 4 to 5 minutes, then open the lid and flip the vegetables and tenderloin pieces. Close the lid and cook for 4 to 5 minutes more. Open the lid and test the internal temperature of the pork with an instant-read thermometer; it should be 145°F.

5. When the pork is done, remove it from the grill and let it rest. Remove the onions and peppers when they are caramelized and set them aside. Slice the pepper quarters into thin strips.

6. Warm the tortillas on the grill for a minute on each side. To build each fajita, layer a couple of pork slices, onions, and red and green peppers slices on top of a warm tortilla and drizzle with crema. Top with crumbled queso fresco and enjoy!

PRO TIP: I like using GrillGrates or a flat-top grill on top of my cooking grate for the vegetables in this recipe so they get nice and caramelized without falling through the grates. Also try serving these with Mesquite Grilled Salsa (page 180).

THICK-CUT PORK STEAK

SERVES 4 TO 5 / **PREP TIME:** 30 minutes / **COOK TIME:** 10 to 15 minutes
SUGGESTED WOOD: Applewood chips

Pork steaks are a very underrated cut. If you cannot find them already cut, you can have your butcher cut a whole bone-in pork shoulder into 1½-inch-thick steaks. Make sure to use a bone-in shoulder so the steaks will hold together better. An average whole pork butt or shoulder should yield four or five steaks.

1 tablespoon salt
4 or 5 (1½-inch-thick)
 pork steaks
2½ tablespoons Sweet
 and Savory Rub
 (page 195)
Southwest Sweet Heat
 BBQ Sauce (page 199),
 to taste

1. Lightly salt both sides of each pork steak and let sit at room temperature for 10 to 15 minutes. I like to keep the fat on this cut, as it will caramelize when cooking and adds great flavor. After 10 to 15 minutes, season both sides with the rub and set aside.

2. Set up your grill for direct cooking (see page 3). Fill a charcoal chimney with charcoal and light it with a fire starter cube. When the coals have turned gray, dump them into the grill grate or basket in an even layer, replace the cooking grate, close the lid, and open the top and bottom vents. You want your grill to be very hot for direct cooking, at least 450°F, before putting any food on it. Right before you plan to cook, scatter a small handful of applewood chips directly on the hot coals.

3. When the grill is up to temperature, place the pork steaks on the cooking grate in an even layer. Close the lid and cook for 2 to 3 minutes. Open the lid, rotate the steaks 90 degrees, close the lid, and cook for another 2 to 3 minutes. Open the lid, flip the steaks, close the lid, and cook for 2 to 3 minutes more. Open the lid and test the internal temperature of the pork steaks; it should be 143°F to 145°F. If they're not there yet, rotate the steaks 90 degrees, then continue to cook until the steaks reach that temperature.

4. When the steaks are done, remove them from the grill to a plate. Brush both sides of each steak with the barbecue sauce and return them to the grill. Open the lid and cook on each side for 1 to 2 minutes, making sure the sauce doesn't burn.

5. Remove the steaks and let rest for 10 to 15 minutes. To serve, plate each steak or slice them into strips and serve with extra barbecue sauce on the side, if desired.

PRO TIP: For pork steaks, rib-eye steak, and venison backstrap, I like to set the meat out at room temperature for at least 30 minutes to an hour after seasoning it. This allows it to sweat and start accepting the salts and flavors deeper into the muscle structures. It also leads to shorter cooking times, which allows me to achieve the internal temperature I'm looking for without burning the exterior.

Bacon and Brie Stuffed Pork Burger

MAKES 6 BURGERS / PREP TIME: 30 to 45 minutes / **COOK TIME:** 10 to 15 minutes
SUGGESTED WOOD: Pecan wood chips

This is my version of the famous "Juicy Lucy" burger but made with ground pork, creamy Brie, and caramelized red onions. It may sound fancy, but you will need several napkins for this burger!

3 pounds ground pork

3 tablespoons SPGJ Rub (page 194)

1 (8-ounce) package Brie cheese

4 to 6 slices Spicy Candied Bacon (page 27), crumbled

1 red onion, sliced into ¼-inch-thick disks

Avocado oil spray

Arugula

1 recipe Smoked Garlic Aioli (page 203)

6 hamburger buns

1. Divide and form the ground pork into 12 equal-size patties and lay them out on a cutting board. Slice the Brie into 6 (1-by-2-inch) rectangles that are ¼ inch thick. Place a Brie slice in the center of 6 of the patties and top each with an equal portion of the crumbled bacon. Place the remaining 6 patties on top of the cheese and bacon, forming the meat around the filling and sealing them well on all sides. Season both sides of the burgers with the rub and set aside. Right before you plan to cook, spray the burgers and the onions with avocado oil to prevent them from sticking to the grill.

2. Set up your grill for direct cooking (see page 4). Fill a charcoal chimney with charcoal and light it with a fire starter cube. When the coals have turned gray, dump them into the grill grate or basket in an even layer, close the lid, and open the top and bottom vents. Right before you plan to cook, scatter a small handful of pecan wood chips directly on the hot coals.

3. When the grill temperature reaches at least 450°F, place the onions and burgers on the cooking grate directly over the coals, close the lid, and cook for 1½ to 2 minutes. Open the lid and give the burgers a 90-degree turn. Close lid and cook for another 1½ to 2 minutes, then open the lid and flip the burgers and onions. Cook for 1½ to 2 minutes more, open the lid, and give the burgers another 90-degree turn. At this point, test the internal temperature of the pork with an instant-read thermometer, making sure not to probe the cheese in the center. You are looking for the pork to reach 158°F to 160°F.

4. When the burgers are done and the onions are caramelized to your liking, remove them from the grill and set aside to rest for 5 to 10 minutes.

5. To build each burger, spread some aioli on a bottom bun, add a burger patty, top with caramelized red onions and some arugula, and add more aioli on top. Cover with the top bun and enjoy!

Sonoran Bacon-Wrapped Pork Hot Dog

MAKES 6 HOT DOGS / **PREP TIME:** 15 to 20 minutes / **COOK TIME:** 8 to 10 minutes
SUGGESTED WOOD: Mesquite lump charcoal

"Sonoran hot dogs" originated in Hermosillo, Mexico, just south of Arizona, and became a street-food favorite in southern Arizona. These hot dogs take me back to my days living in Tucson, Arizona, when I just got out of the US Navy. My wife and I would go out for the night, and the Sonoran dog vendor just outside of the club was a welcome sight after several beverages. You are going to need two hands to eat this beast!

6 thin bacon slices

6 all-pork hot dogs

1 (16-ounce) can pinto beans

1 Roma tomato, diced

1 small white onion, diced

1 bunch cilantro, chopped

1 small jalapeño, seeded and finely diced

Juice of 1 lime

Salt

Freshly ground black pepper

6 soft bolillo rolls

½ cup mayonnaise

½ cup crumbled cotija Cheese

1. Wrap a slice of bacon around each hot dog and set them aside. In a saucepan, warm the beans over medium heat. (I like to put them on my grill in a grill-safe pan to pick up some smoke and added flavor.)

2. To make the pico de gallo, combine the tomato, onion, cilantro, jalapeño, and lime juice in a bowl. Season with salt and pepper to taste. Cover and refrigerate this mixture until you're ready to serve.

3. Set up your grill for direct cooking (see page 3). Fill a charcoal chimney with mesquite lump charcoal and light it with a fire starter cube. When the coals have turned gray, dump them into the grill grate or basket in an even layer, close the lid, and open the top and bottom vents.

4. When the grill temperature reaches at least 450°F, place the dogs on the cooking grate directly over the coals, close the lid, and cook for 1½ to 2 minutes. Open the lid and give the dogs a quarter turn, then close lid. After another 1½ to 2 minutes, open the lid and give them another quarter turn, then close the lid and cook for 1½ to 2 minutes more. Open the lid and give them another quarter turn. At this point you are looking for the bacon to be cooked through and the fat to be rendered.

5. Remove the dogs from the grill and set aside to rest for 5 to 10 minutes.

6. To build the Sonoran dog, cut the bolillo roll down the center and spread it with some mayonnaise. Place a dog in the middle and top it with a couple of spoonfuls of warm pinto beans. Top with pico de gallo, crumbled cotija cheese, and a drizzle of mayonnaise over the top.

> **PRO TIP:** I like to use thin-cut bacon for these dogs. The fat will render faster than thick-cut bacon, leaving the hot dog nice and juicy inside.

Chapter 5

POULTRY AND GAME BIRDS

◀ Huli-Huli Style Chicken (page 114)

"Fried" Buttermilk Chicken Legs

SERVES 4 TO 6 / PREP TIME: 30 to 45 minutes, plus 8 hours to marinate
COOK TIME: 30 to 45 minutes / **SUGGESTED WOOD:** Applewood chunks

I love making "fried" food on my grill. The key is high heat and using spray oil to help create the crispy texture you get from fried foods. You will need to run your grill a little hotter, but you'll still set it up for indirect cooking.

6 to 10 chicken legs (thighs and drumsticks)
2 cups buttermilk
2 large eggs, beaten
1 tablespoon hot sauce
2½ cups all-purpose flour
¼ cup Poultry and Seafood Rub (page 196)
1 teaspoon salt
1 teaspoon freshly ground black pepper
1 teaspoon red pepper flakes
Avocado oil spray
Classic White BBQ Sauce (page 200), to taste

1. Using a sharp knife, make a ½-inch-deep slit in the side of each chicken leg parallel to the bone. In a large glass bowl or resealable plastic bag, combine the buttermilk, beaten eggs, and hot sauce. Add the legs, massaging or tossing them in the marinade, cover (or seal the bag), and refrigerate at least 8 hours or up to overnight.

2. Place a wire rack on top of a foil-lined baking sheet. Remove the legs from the marinade (discarding it) and lay the legs on the wire rack.

3. In a large resealable bag, combine the flour, rub, salt, black pepper, and red pepper flakes and toss to incorporate. Add the legs, 2 or 3 at a time, to the flour mixture, seal the bag, and toss to coat the legs thoroughly. Lay the breaded legs back on the wire rack and repeat with the remaining legs.

4. Set up your grill for indirect cooking (see page 4). Fill a charcoal chimney with lump charcoal and light it with a fire starter cube. When the coals have turned gray, dump them into the grill on the side opposite the disposable aluminum pan, replace the cooking grate, close the lid, and open the top and bottom vents until the grill temperature registers about 325°F. Continue to

monitor the grill, adjusting the vents as needed, until it reaches a cooking temperature of 350°F to 375°F. About 15 minutes before you plan to cook, place 1 or 2 medium applewood chunks directly on the hot coals, then close the lid.

5. When the grill is ready, spray both sides of the chicken legs with avocado oil. Open the lid and place the legs on the indirect side, close the lid, and cook for 15 minutes. Open the lid, flip the legs, and cook for another 10 to 15 minutes. You are looking for the legs to turn golden brown and reach an internal temperature of at least 165°F.

6. When the legs have reached your desired doneness, remove them from the grill and let rest for 10 to 15 minutes. Place them on a serving platter, drizzle with white sauce, and enjoy.

PRO TIP: I like to cook chicken legs a little longer and remove them when they are a nice golden brown and have an internal temperature of 185°F to 190°F. I find the longer cooking time leads to a more tender bite and crispier crust.

Herb Butter Smoked Turkey Breast

SERVES 4 TO 6 / **PREP TIME:** 30 minutes, plus overnight brine / **COOK TIME:** 2½ to 3 hours
SUGGESTED WOOD: Applewood chunks

I have taught this recipe on several occasions in my holiday barbecue classes, and it is a winner every time. The brine keeps the meat juicy and moist, and the herb butter is perfect for making that golden brown skin. I also like cooking the breast by itself; I can concentrate on getting the internal temperature just right without worrying about the legs or thighs being up to proper temperature.

1 (5- to 6-pound) whole bone-in turkey breast, skin on
Poultry and Seafood Herb Brine (page 202), cooled, as needed
1 cup (2 sticks) unsalted butter, softened
1 tablespoon Italian seasoning
1 tablespoon Poultry and Seafood Rub (page 196)
1 tablespoon chopped fresh rosemary
1 teaspoon garlic powder
1 teaspoon freshly ground black pepper
Butter-flavored vegetable oil spray

1. Trim any excess fat or hanging skin from the turkey breast. Pour the cooled brine into a large bowl or resealable bag, then add the turkey breast, making sure it's completely submerged, and refrigerate it overnight.

2. Place a wire rack on top of a foil-lined baking sheet. Remove the turkey from the brine, shake off any excess liquid, and discard the leftover brine. Lay the turkey breast on the wire rack and pat it dry with paper towels. Make sure the turkey is dry and sits for a few minutes at room temperature before using the butter.

3. Make the herb butter in a mixing bowl by combining the softened butter, Italian seasoning, the rub, rosemary, garlic powder, and pepper and stir to blend thoroughly.

4. Rub three-quarters of the herb butter mixture all over the turkey breast, both over and under the skin.

5. Set up your grill for indirect cooking (see page 4). Fill a charcoal chimney with lump charcoal and light it with a fire starter cube. When the coals have turned gray, dump them into the grill on the side opposite the disposable aluminum pan, replace the cooking grate, close the lid, and open the top and bottom vents until the grill temperature registers about 300°F. Continue

to monitor the grill, adjusting the vents as needed, until it reaches a cooking temperature of 325°F to 350°F. About 15 minutes before you plan to cook, place 1 or 2 medium applewood chunks directly on the hot coals, then close the lid.

6. When the grill is ready, open the lid and place the turkey breast on the indirect side, close the lid, and cook for 1 hour. Open the lid, spray the turkey with spray butter, rotate the turkey 180 degrees, and cook for another hour.

7. After 2 hours, open the lid, spray the turkey again with butter, and rotate it another 180 degrees. At this time, check the internal temperature with an instant-read thermometer; you are looking for 163°F to 165°F. Continue to cook and spray with butter until the breast reaches this temperature.

8. Remove the turkey from the grill to a plate. Spoon the remainder of the herb butter over the turkey, cover loosely with aluminum foil, and let rest for 15 to 20 minutes. When you're ready to eat, move the turkey to a cutting board, carve it into slices, and spoon the melted herb butter from the resting plate over the slices before serving.

PRO TIP: I like to use a butter-flavored spray, especially when cooking turkey, chicken, and Cornish hens. The butter helps the skin render the fat below and gives it a beautiful golden color.

WHOLE SMOKED CORNISH GAME HENS

SERVES 4 TO 6 / **PREP TIME:** 30 minutes, plus overnight brine / **COOK TIME:** 1 to 1½ hours
SUGGESTED WOOD: Pecan wood chunks

These whole Cornish hens are perfect for a family gathering, as each person is served their own whole hen. Brining them overnight will lead to a more flavorful, moist, and tender product, especially because you are cooking them whole. It is sometimes hard to get the white meat and dark meat perfect when cooking whole birds, but the brine will allow you to push the internal temperature a bit higher to get the thighs and legs just right while maintaining moisture in the breast.

4 to 6 whole Cornish game hens, trimmed of excess fat

Poultry and Seafood Herb Brine (page 202), cooled, as needed

2 small oranges, cut into eighths, plus extra slices for garnish

2 small onions, cut into eighths

6 fresh sage leaves, chopped, plus more for garnish

6 garlic cloves, chopped

4 to 5 tablespoons Poultry and Seafood Rub (page 196)

Butter-flavored vegetable oil spray

1. Make sure to empty the cavity of each hen. Pour the cooled brine into a large bowl or resealable bag, then add the hens, making sure they are completely submerged. You might have to use a second bowl or bag, or make a double batch of the brine. Refrigerate overnight.

2. Place a wire rack on top of a foil-lined baking sheet. Remove the hens, shake off the excess liquid, and discard the leftover brine. Lay the hens on the wire rack and pat them dry with paper towels. Make sure they are as dry as possible.

3. In a mixing bowl, combine the orange and onion wedges with the chopped sage and garlic. Divide and place this mixture evenly into each hen's cavity, then season the hens all over with the rub. Set aside.

4. Set up your grill for indirect cooking (see page 4). Fill a charcoal chimney with lump charcoal and light it with a fire starter cube. When the coals have turned gray, dump them into the grill on the side opposite the disposable aluminum pan, replace the cooking grate, close the lid, and open the top and bottom vents until the grill temperature registers about 300°F. Continue to monitor the grill, adjusting the vents as needed, until

it reaches a cooking temperature of 325°F to 350°F. About 15 minutes before you plan to cook, place 1 or 2 medium pecan wood chunks directly on the hot coals, then close the lid.

5. When the grill is ready, open the lid and place the hens on the indirect side, close the lid, and cook for 30 to 45 minutes. Open the lid, spray the hens with spray butter, rotate them 180 degrees, close the lid, and cook for another 30 to 45 minutes. Open the lid and test for doneness (163°F to 165°F) with an instant-read thermometer. Continue to cook, rotate, and spray with butter until this temperature is reached.

6. When done, remove the hens from the grill to a plate, cover loosely with aluminum foil, and let rest for 15 to 20 minutes.

7. To serve, place the hens on a large serving tray and garnish with orange slices and chopped fresh sage.

PRO TIP: Try using the glaze from my Duck Breast with Sweet and Spicy Orange Glaze (page 112) on these hens. I think the glaze pairs well with all the flavors involved and adds a nice sweetness.

CREAMY JALAPEÑO TURKEY BURGER

MAKES 4 TO 6 BURGERS / **PREP TIME:** 30 to 45 minutes / **COOK TIME:** 10 to 12 minutes
SUGGESTED WOOD: Applewood chips

Burgers are a weekly go-to for our family, and as much as we love ground beef burgers, we also love using other ground proteins like turkey, especially for burger night.

**2 to 3 pounds
ground turkey**

**3 tablespoons Poultry and
Seafood Rub (page 196)**

Avocado oil spray

8 ounces cream cheese

**1 recipe Smoked Garlic
Aioli (page 203)**

**4 to 6 soft potato
hamburger buns**

**1 (16-ounce) jar or can
pickled jalapeño
slices, drained**

**Fried onion straws, such
as French's Original
Crispy Fried Onions,
for serving**

1. Divide and form the turkey into 4 to 6 equal-size patties. Season both sides with the rub, spray with avocado oil, and set aside.

2. Set up your grill for direct cooking (see page 3). Fill a charcoal chimney with charcoal and light it with a fire starter cube. When the coals have turned gray, dump them into the grill grate or basket in an even layer, close the lid, and open the top and bottom vents; you are looking for a hot fire and a grill temperature at least 450°F. Right before you plan to cook, scatter a small handful of applewood chips directly on the hot coals.

3. Place the burger patties on the grate directly over the coals and cook for 1½ to 2 minutes, then give the patties a 90-degree turn and close the lid. After another 1½ to 2 minutes, open the lid and give the burgers a flip, then close the lid and cook for 1½ to 2 minutes more. Open the lid and give the burgers a final 90-degree turn. Test for doneness (163°F to 165°F) with an instant-read thermometer. Place 1 to 2 ounces of cream cheese on top of each patty and close the lid. After 1 to 2 minutes, or when your desired doneness is reached and the cream cheese is melted, remove the burgers to a plate and let rest for 5 to 10 minutes.

4. To build each burger, spoon some aioli on both sides of a bun. Place the burger patty on the bottom bun, add pickled jalapeños on top of the cream cheese, and top with onion straws. Cover with the top bun and enjoy!

BACON-WRAPPED CHICKEN WINGS

SERVES 4 TO 6 / **PREP TIME:** 15 to 20 minutes / **COOK TIME:** 1 hour
SUGGESTED WOOD: Pecan wood chunks

These wings are inspired by my good barbecue friend Kyle Matuszewski from Your Behind BBQ. He has won several competitions with his bacon-wrapped chicken wings. This is my version, without giving away too many of his championship secrets.

12 to 15 chicken wings,
flats and drums
separated
1 (12-ounce) package
thin-sliced bacon
3 to 4 tablespoons
Sweet and Savory Rub
(page 195)
Southwest Sweet Heat
BBQ Sauce (page 199),
to taste
3 carrots, sliced
3 celery stalks, sliced
Smoked Garlic Aioli
(page 203), for serving

1. Pat the wings dry with a paper towel. Wrap each wing in a slice of bacon, securing it with a toothpick if needed. Season them with the rub and set aside.

2. Set up your grill for indirect cooking (see page 4). Fill a charcoal chimney with lump charcoal and light it with a fire starter cube. When the coals have turned gray, dump them into the grill on the side opposite the disposable aluminum pan, replace the cooking grate, close the lid, and open the top and bottom vents until the grill temperature registers about 300°F. Continue to monitor the grill, adjusting the vents as needed, until it reaches a cooking temperature of 325°F to 350°F. About 15 minutes before you plan to cook, place 1 or 2 medium pecan wood chunks directly on the hot coals, then close the lid.

3. When the grill is up to temperature, place the chicken wings on the indirect side, close the lid, and cook for 30 minutes. Open the lid, flip the wings, close the lid, and cook for 20 minutes more, or until the bacon is cooked and the wings' internal temperature is at least 165°F.

4. During the last 1 to 2 minutes of cooking, brush the wings with barbecue sauce and finish them over direct heat to caramelize the sauce. Remove the wings from the grill when done and set aside to rest for 5 to 10 minutes. Serve the wings with carrot and celery slices and the aioli.

Duck Breast with Sweet and Spicy Orange Glaze

SERVES 4 TO 6 / **PREP TIME:** 30 to 45 minutes / **COOK TIME:** 15 to 20 minutes
SUGGESTED WOOD: Cherrywood chips

Duck breast is a very lean protein and can dry out at higher internal temperatures. Keeping the internal temperature between 135°F and 140°F will give you the juiciest, most flavorful product. Duck pairs well with sweet flavor profiles, so I like to use this sweet orange glaze that has a nice light, spicy kick. You can adjust your heat level by adding more or less red pepper flakes and sriracha.

For the glaze
¾ cup orange juice
¼ cup packed light
  brown sugar
¼ cup soy sauce
2 tablespoons honey
2 or 3 garlic
  cloves, minced
1 teaspoon red
  pepper flakes
1 teaspoon sriracha

For the duck
2 (8- to 10-ounce)
  boneless duck
  breasts, skin on
1½ tablespoons SPGJ Rub
  (page 194)
Avocado oil spray
Orange slices, for garnish

1. **TO MAKE THE GLAZE:** In a saucepan over medium heat, combine all ingredients for the glaze. Stir to combine and bring to a low, slow boil while stirring. Once it boils, reduce the heat to medium-low and stir for 5 to 6 minutes, until it starts to thicken, then remove the pan from the heat and set aside. The glaze will thicken upon standing.

2. **TO COOK THE DUCK:** Score the fatty side of the duck breasts in a crosshatch pattern. Do not cut deep into the meat, just to where it meets the fat line. Sprinkle both sides of the duck with the rub and set aside.

3. Set up your grill for direct cooking (see page 3). Fill a charcoal chimney with charcoal and light it with a fire starter cube. When the coals have turned gray, dump them into the grill grate or basket in an even layer, close the lid, replace the cooking grate, and open the top and bottom vents until the grill thermometer registers at least 450°F (this can take 20 to 30 minutes). Right before you plan to cook, scatter a small handful of cherrywood chips directly on the hot coals.

4. When the grill is ready, spray the duck breasts with avocado oil, then lay them fat-side down on the grill. Close the lid and cook for 5 to 6 minutes. Open the lid, rotate the duck 90 degrees, close the lid, and cook for another 5 to 6 minutes. Open the lid, flip the duck breasts over, close the lid, and cook for 2 to 3 minutes. Open the lid, rotate the duck 90 degrees, and test the internal temperature (which should be 135°F to 140°F when done). During the last 2 to 3 minutes of cooking, or when the breast is about 130°F, brush it with the orange glaze, then flip and cook for 1 to 2 minutes. Brush it again, then flip to cook for another 1 to 2 minutes, or until it reaches your desired doneness.

5. Remove the breasts from the grill and lay them on a plate, cover loosely with aluminum foil, and let rest for 10 to 15 minutes. To serve, lay the breasts on a cutting board and slice them into ½-inch strips. Garnish with orange slices and serve with extra orange glaze on the side.

PRO TIP: Much like venison, duck breast is best served medium-rare to medium. At higher temperatures, it tends to dry out and won't be as flavorful.

HULI-HULI STYLE CHICKEN

SERVES 6 TO 8 / PREP TIME: 8 hours to overnight / **COOK TIME:** 1 to 1½ hours
SUGGESTED WOOD: Hickory wood chunks

I was stationed in Pearl Harbor, Hawaii, during my service in the US Navy, and there was a little Hawaiian barbecue shack we would frequently visit. The smell from the half chickens turning over kiawe wood was sweet and smoky, like no other smell on earth, and you could hear the sizzle as the chicken fat hit the coals beneath. This recipe is inspired by that barbecue shack, and I know once you try it, it will be a family favorite of yours, too.

1 whole chicken,
   split into halves,
   backbone removed
½ cup soy sauce
2 cups Sticky Honey
   Teriyaki Sauce
   (page 198),
   chilled, divided
½ cup diced pineapple
2 or 3 scallions, sliced

1. Pat the chicken halves dry with a paper towel. With a sharp knife, make two slits about ½ inch deep and 2 inches long, one in the leg/thigh area and one in the largest part of the breast.

2. In a large glass mixing bowl or resealable bag, combine the soy sauce and 1 cup (one batch) of chilled teriyaki sauce. Add the chicken halves and turn to coat them evenly. Cover or seal and refrigerate at least 8 hours or overnight.

3. Place a wire rack on top of a foil-lined baking sheet. After marinating, remove the chicken and discard the leftover marinade. Lay the chicken out on the wire rack to dry out while you get the grill ready.

4. Set up your grill for indirect cooking (see page 4). Fill a charcoal chimney with lump charcoal and light it with a fire starter cube. When the coals have turned gray, dump them into the grill on the side opposite the disposable aluminum pan, replace the cooking grate, close the lid, and open the top and bottom vents until the grill temperature registers about 300°F. Continue to monitor the grill, adjusting the vents as needed, until it reaches a cooking temperature of 325°F to 350°F. About 15 minutes before you plan to cook, place 1 or

2 medium hickory wood chunks directly on the hot coals, then close the lid.

5. When the grill is up to temperature, place the chicken halves, skin-side up, on the indirect side of the grill over the drip pan, close the lid, and cook for 25 to 30 minutes. Open the lid and *huli*, or "flip," the chicken halves over, close the lid, and cook for another 25 to 30 minutes. After 50 minutes to 1 hour, open the lid and test the internal temperature in the thigh area and breast. When the chicken is about 160°F, move it to the direct side of the grill, skin-side down, and brush it with ¼ cup of teriyaki sauce. Cook for 2 to 3 minutes with the lid off, flip the chicken halves, brush them again with another ¼ cup of sauce, and cook for 2 to 3 minutes. Test the internal temperature to make sure it is at least 165°F.

6. When the chicken is done, remove it from the grill to a plate, and let it rest for 10 to 15 minutes, loosely covered with aluminum foil. When ready to serve, place the chicken halves on a serving plate, top with diced pineapple, sliced scallions, and a drizzle of teriyaki sauce Serve with the remaining teriyaki sauce on the side.

PRO TIP: Serve this chicken with Hawaiian Mac Salad (page 170). The contrast in the creamy salad and the sweet, sticky, charred chicken is an amazing combination of flavors.

Brined Turkey BLT Sandwich (TBLT)

SERVES 4 TO 6 / PREP TIME: 30 minutes, plus overnight brine / COOK TIME: 1 to 1½ hours
SUGGESTED WOOD: Applewood chunks

This is my take on the classic BLT sandwich with the addition of a smoked, juicy turkey breast and creamy avocado. Brining the turkey breast overnight in the Poultry and Seafood Herb Brine adds flavor and will help retain moisture while smoking.

1 (3- to 4-pound) whole
    turkey breast, boneless
    and skinless
Poultry and Seafood
    Herb Brine (page 202),
    cooled, as needed
1 tablespoon Poultry and
    Seafood Rub (page 196)
Butter-flavored spray
2 to 3 tablespoons
    salted butter
8 to 12 slices sourdough
    bread or Texas toast
Mayonnaise, preferably
    Duke's, for topping
8 to 12 slices Spicy
    Candied Bacon (page 27)
2 avocados, pitted,
    peeled, and sliced
1 head iceberg lettuce,
    shredded
2 Roma tomatoes, sliced

1. Trim any excess fat from the turkey. Pour the cooled brine into a large bowl or resealable bag and add the turkey, making sure it is submerged. Cover or seal and refrigerate overnight.

2. Place a wire rack on top of a foil-lined baking sheet. After brining, remove the turkey, shake off any excess liquid, and discard the leftover brine. Lay the breast on the wire rack and pat it as dry as possible with paper towels. Season all sides lightly with the rub and set it aside.

3. Set up your grill for indirect cooking (see page 4). Fill a charcoal chimney with lump charcoal and light it with a fire starter cube. When the coals have turned gray, dump them into the grill on the side opposite the disposable aluminum pan, replace the cooking grate, close the lid, and open the top and bottom vents until the grill temperature registers about 275°F. Continue to monitor the grill, adjusting the vents as needed, until it reaches a cooking temperature of 300°F to 325°F. About 15 minutes before you plan to cook, place 1 or 2 medium applewood chunks directly on the hot coals, then close the lid.

4. When the grill is ready, place the turkey breast on the indirect side, close the lid, and cook for 30 to 45 minutes. Open the lid, spray the breast with spray butter, rotate it 180 degrees, close the lid, and cook for another 30 to 45 minutes. Open the lid and, using an instant-read thermometer, test for doneness (163°F to 165°F). Continue to cook, rotate, and spray with butter until the temperature is reached.

5. When done, remove the turkey breast from the grill to a plate. Spread the butter on top of the turkey breast, cover loosely with aluminum foil, and let rest for 15 to 20 minutes.

6. While the turkey is resting, coat one side of each bread slice with mayonnaise and place, mayo-side down, on a flat-top grill or directly over the coals to toast. Remove when golden brown and toasty on one side, making sure not to burn them.

7. Place the turkey on a cutting board and slice it thinly. Place the sliced turkey back on the resting plate in the reserved butter and juices.

8. To build your sandwich, spread mayonnaise to the untoasted side of each bread slice. Top with thin sliced turkey, 2 slices of bacon, sliced avocado, shredded lettuce, and tomatoes and cover with another slice of toasted bread. Serve and enjoy!

BACON-WRAPPED MOZZARELLA-STUFFED BONELESS CHICKEN THIGHS

SERVES 4 TO 6 / PREP TIME: 30 to 45 minutes / **COOK TIME:** 35 to 45 minutes
SUGGESTED WOOD: Pecan wood chunks

These bacon-wrapped chicken thighs are also known as chicken bombs because they explode with flavor when you bite into them. I like using boneless, skinless thighs, which retain more moisture and have more flavor than white meat chicken. Make sure to tightly wrap the thighs with thin-sliced bacon for best results.

8 to 12 boneless, skinless chicken thighs

½ cup mayonnaise

2 tablespoons Poultry and Seafood Rub (page 196)

4 to 6 mozzarella string cheese sticks

1 (12-ounce) package thin-sliced bacon

1. Pat the chicken thighs dry with a paper towel to remove any excess moisture and lay them on a cutting board. Lightly brush mayonnaise on both sides of the thighs and sprinkle with the rub. Halve each string cheese crosswise and place one half in the center of each chicken thigh. Roll the thigh around the cheese, then wrap a strip of bacon around the thigh. Secure the ends with a toothpick. Repeat the process with the remaining chicken thighs, string cheese, and bacon. Lightly sprinkle the outside of each thigh with the rub. Set aside.

2. Set up your grill for indirect cooking (see page 4). Fill a charcoal chimney with lump charcoal and light it with a fire starter cube. When the coals have turned gray, dump them into the grill on the side opposite the disposable aluminum pan, replace the cooking grate, close the lid, and open the top and bottom vents until the grill temperature registers about 275°F. Continue to monitor the grill, adjusting the vents as needed, until it reaches a cooking temperature of 300°F to 325°F. About 15 minutes before you plan to cook, place 1 or

2 medium pecan wood chunks directly on the hot coals, then close the lid.

3. When the grill is ready, place the thighs on the indirect side, close the lid, and cook for 20 minutes. Open the lid, rotate the thighs 180 degrees, close the lid, and cook for another 15 to 20 minutes. Open the lid and, using an instant-read thermometer, test the thigh for doneness (163°F to 165°F). Continue to cook and rotate until the temperature is reached and the bacon is cooked through.

4. When done, remove the thighs from the grill to a plate to rest for 10 to 15 minutes, covered loosely with aluminum foil.

5. After resting, remove the toothpicks and place the thighs on a cutting board. Slice them in half, serve, and enjoy!

PRO TIP: Brush some Southwest Sweet Heat BBQ Sauce (page 199) on the thighs during the last 2 to 3 minutes of cooking, moving them to the direct side of the grill to caramelize for an added layer of flavor.

Spatchcocked BBQ Chicken

SERVES 4 TO 6 / PREP TIME: 30 minutes, plus overnight brine
COOK TIME: 1½ to 2 hours / **SUGGESTED WOOD:** Pecan wood chunks

When I cook poultry at home, I like to spatchcock the bird to open up more surface area that smoke can reach for flavor. It also contributes to a more evenly cooked bird. The process is easy and only takes a few minutes with a good pair of kitchen shears. *(Photograph on page ii.)*

1 (4- to 5-pound)
  whole chicken
**Poultry and Seafood
  Herb Brine (page 202),**
  chilled, as needed
1¼ tablespoons **Poultry
  and Seafood Rub
  (page 196)**
Avocado oil spray
**Southwest Sweet Heat
  BBQ Sauce (page 199),**
  to taste

1. Lay the chicken on a cutting board and pat it dry with paper towels. To remove the backbone, use a pair of kitchen shears to cut parallel to the backbone on either side of it. Discard the backbone or save it for making stock. Lay the chicken skin-side up, then gently but firmly push down in the center of the breast to crack the breast-bone so the chicken lies flat. In a large bowl or resealable bag, cover the chicken with the brine, cover, and refrigerate for at least 8 hours or up to overnight.

2. Place a wire rack on a foil-lined baking sheet. Remove the chicken from the brine, let the excess drip off, and discard the leftover brine. Lay the chicken on the wire rack and pat both sides dry with paper towels. Sprinkle both sides lightly with the rub and set aside.

3. Set up your grill for indirect cooking (see page 4). Fill a charcoal chimney with lump charcoal and light it with a fire starter cube. When the coals have turned gray, dump them into the grill on the side opposite the disposable aluminum pan, replace the cooking grate, close the lid, and open the top and bottom vents until the grill temperature registers about 300°F. Continue to monitor the grill, adjusting the vents as needed, until it reaches a cooking temperature of 325°F to 350°F. About 15 minutes before you plan to cook, place 1 or 2 medium pecan wood chunks directly on the hot coals, then close the lid.

4. When the grill is ready, spray the chicken with avo-cado oil, open the lid, and place the chicken skin-side up on the indirect side. Close the lid and cook for 45 minutes. Open the lid, flip the chicken, close the lid, and cook for another 45 minutes. Open the lid and, using an instant-read thermometer, test for doneness (160°F to 163°F). Continue to cook and flip until temperature is reached.

5. When the chicken is about 5°F from your desired doneness, brush the skin side with barbecue sauce and move it to the direct side of the grill, skin-side over the coals. Brush the bone side with more sauce, cook for 2 to 3 minutes to caramelize the sauce, then flip it over. Cook for 1 to 2 minutes more until the breast meat reaches 165°F.

6. When the chicken is done, remove it from the grill to a plate, loosely cover with aluminum foil, and let rest for 10 to 15 minutes. After resting, move the chicken to a cutting board and carve the legs, thighs, breast, and wings. Serve and enjoy!

PRO TIP: For crispier chicken skin, cook it at a higher temperature and finish it skin-side down over the hot side of the grill for a few minutes to render the fat beneath the skin.

CHICKEN YAKITORI SKEWERS

SERVES 6 TO 8 / **PREP TIME:** 10 to 15 minutes / **COOK TIME:** 10 to 15 minutes
SUGGESTED WOOD: Maple wood chips

Skewered meat cooked directly over hot coals is a popular dish in pretty much every part of the world. My travels during my service in the US Navy and beyond have led me all around the Pacific Ocean and other parts of this amazing planet. These skewers remind me specifically of journeys through eastern Asia and the Middle East. The sizzle of the meat over the grill and the sweet, sticky sauce caramelized on the outside make this dish a weekly go-to in our family. Serve them with Hawaiian Mac Salad (page 170) for an authentic Hawaiian-style meal.

6 to 8 boneless, skinless chicken thighs, cut into 1-inch cubes

Salt

Freshly ground black pepper

Avocado oil spray

1 cup Sticky Honey Teriyaki Sauce (page 198), divided

1 tablespoon toasted sesame seeds

2 to 3 scallions, sliced

1. Skewer the cubed chicken thighs onto six to eight wood or metal skewers. Season them lightly with salt and pepper and set aside.

2. Set up your grill for direct cooking (see page 3). Fill a charcoal chimney with charcoal and light it with a fire starter cube. When the coals have turned gray, dump them into the grill grate or basket in an even layer, close the lid, replace the cooking grate, and open the top and bottom vents until the grill thermometer registers at least 450°F (this can take 20 to 30 minutes). Right before you plan to cook, scatter a small handful of maple wood chips directly on the hot coals and spray the chicken skewers with avocado oil.

3. When the grill is up to temperature, place the chicken skewers over the coals evenly around the grill. Close the lid and cook for 1 to 2 minutes. Open the lid and give the skewers a quarter turn, close the lid, and cook

for another 1 to 2 minutes. Open the lid, give the skewers another quarter turn, and cook for 1 to 2 minutes more. After 1 to 2 minutes, open the lid and test the internal temperature of the thighs. When the chicken reaches 162°F to 163°F, brush it with ¼ cup of teriyaki sauce. Cook for 2 to 3 minutes (with the lid off if you're using a charcoal grill), flip the skewers, brush them again with ¼ cup of teriyaki sauce, and cook for 2 to 3 minutes more. At this point, test the internal temperature to make sure it is at least 165°F before removing the thighs from the grill.

4. Place the cooked thighs on a plate and let rest for 5 to 10 minutes, loosely covered with aluminum foil. When ready to serve, place the skewers on a serving plate and top with toasted sesame seeds and sliced scallions. Serve with the remaining teriyaki sauce on the side.

PRO TIP: If you're using wooden skewers, make sure to soak them in water for 20 minutes prior to using so they don't burn on the grill.

MARINATED PULLED QUAIL TOSTADA

SERVES 4 TO 6 / PREP TIME: 8 hours to overnight / COOK TIME: 1 to 1½ hours
SUGGESTED WOOD: Mesquite lump charcoal

Quail may not be available at your local grocery store, but many local butcher shops have it readily available. I like to get a good char on these and then braise them so they shred apart easily.

6 (5- to 6-ounce)
   quail halves
2 cups Carne and Pollo
   Asada Marinade
   (page 201)
1¾ tablespoons
   Southwestern
   Seasoning (page 197)
Avocado oil spray
1 cup chicken stock
1 (10-ounce) can diced
   tomatoes and green
   chiles, such as Rotel,
   with their juices
1 jalapeño, diced
1 (16-ounce) can
   refried beans
4 to 6 taco-size corn
   tortillas
Crumbled cotija cheese,
   for serving
1 head iceberg lettuce,
   shredded
2 avocados, pitted,
   peeled, and sliced
Mexican crema, for serving
½ cup chopped fresh
   cilantro, for serving

1. Pat the quail halves dry with a paper towel. Pour the marinade into a large bowl or resealable bag and submerge the quail halves. You may have to use more than one bowl or bag or double the marinade. Cover and refrigerate at least 8 hours or overnight.

2. Place a wire rack on top of a foil-lined baking sheet. Remove the quail, discard the marinade, and lay them on the wire rack. Pat them dry with paper towels and season both sides lightly with the seasoning mix. Spray both sides with avocado oil and set aside.

3. Set up your grill for indirect cooking (see page 4). Fill a charcoal chimney with mesquite lump charcoal and light it with a fire starter cube. When the coals have turned gray, dump them into the grill on the side opposite the disposable aluminum pan, replace the cooking grate, close the lid, and open the top and bottom vents until the grill temperature registers about 300°F. Continue to monitor, adjusting the vents as needed, until it reaches a cooking temperature of 325°F to 350°F.

4. When the grill is up to temperature, place the quail halves skin-side down directly over the coals on the hot side. Close the lid and cook for 5 to 6 minutes. Open the lid, flip the quail halves, and cook for another 5 to 6 minutes. You are looking for both sides to have a nice char, but not to the point of burning. When they have a good char on both sides, move them to the indirect side

and place a Dutch oven or disposable aluminum pan on the grill over the direct side. Place the quail halves in the pan or Dutch oven and add the chicken stock, diced tomatoes and chiles, and jalapeño. Cover with the lid or foil place the pan back on the grill. If you're using a Dutch oven, place it on the direct side; place a disposable pan on the indirect side. Close the lid and cook for 45 minutes to 1 hour.

PRO TIP: I like to add the beans to a small loaf-size aluminum pan and put them on the grill while the quail is braising to pick up some smoky flavor. These tostadas are also delicious with Mesquite Grilled Salsa (page 180).

5. Meanwhile, warm the beans in a saucepan over medium heat; when heated through, turn the heat to low and cover until ready to serve.

6. Check the quail for doneness. You are looking for the quail meat to pull easily and cleanly off the bones. When done, take the Dutch oven or pan off the grill. Carefully remove the quail halves and place them on a cutting board. While they are resting, spray both sides of the tortillas with avocado oil and place them on the indirect side of the grill, close the lid, and cook for 1 to 2 minutes, until they start to firm up a bit. Flip and repeat. You want the tortillas to harden a bit and become crispy. You can move them to the hot side of the grill to crisp up at the end; just make sure not to burn them. Remove the tortillas and set aside.

7. With two forks or gloved hands, remove the meat from the quail halves and discard the skin and bones. Shred all the quail meat into a bowl and add a spoonful or two of the braising liquid left in the pan to keep it moist.

8. To build your tostada, spread a spoonful of refried beans on a crispy tortilla. Sprinkle with some cotija cheese, add some pulled quail, shredded lettuce, sliced avocado, and more crumbled cotija, and drizzle with crema. Top with a pinch of cilantro and serve.

Apple, Sausage, and Sage Stuffed Turkey Tenderloins

SERVES 4 TO 6 / **PREP TIME:** 20 to 30 minutes / **COOK TIME:** 35 to 40 minutes
SUGGESTED WOOD: Applewood chunks

This recipe is inspired by my great friend Leslie Roark Scott from Ubons Restaurant out of Yazoo City, Mississippi. She made this on stage at one of the barbecue festivals we were hosting, and it was my favorite from the event. I love how all the flavors work with the turkey; fatty sausage, crisp apples, and earthy sage are the perfect filling for this lean cut.

1 pound ground
   breakfast sausage

2 tablespoons
   salted butter

1 large Granny Smith
   apple, cored and diced

1 (1-ounce) package fresh
   sage leaves

2 (12- to 16-ounce) turkey
   tenderloins

1¼ tablespoons Poultry
   and Seafood Rub
   (page 196)

Avocado oil spray

1. In a saucepan over medium heat, crumble the breakfast sausage and add the butter. Cook for 5 to 6 minutes, until the sausage is almost done. Add the diced apple and sage leaves and cook over medium to medium-high heat for another 5 to 6 minutes, until the sage leaves start to crumble. When the sausage is cooked through and the sage is dry, remove the pan from the heat and set aside to cool.

2. Pat the tenderloins dry with a paper towel. With a sharp knife, butterfly the tenderloins, cutting them horizontally through the middle and opening them up. Place a large piece of plastic wrap over the tenderloins and lightly pound the meat. Spread half the cooled sausage-apple mixture down the center of one of the tenderloins and roll it up around the filling into a tube shape. With butcher's twine, truss the tenderloins in 1- to 1½-inch increments so it doesn't fall apart while cooking. Season the outside with the rub and set aside. Repeat with the other tenderloin and the remaining sausage-apple mixture.

3. Set up your grill for indirect cooking (see page 4). Fill a charcoal chimney with lump charcoal and light it with a fire starter cube. When the coals have turned gray, dump them into the grill on the side opposite the disposable aluminum pan, replace the cooking grate, close the lid, and open the top and bottom vents until the grill temperature registers about 300°F. Continue to monitor the grill, adjusting the vents as needed, until it reaches a cooking temperature of 325°F to 350°F. About 15 minutes before you plan to cook, place 1 or 2 medium applewood chunks directly on the hot coals, then close the lid.

4. When the grill is up to temperature, spray the tenderloins with avocado oil and place them on the indirect side of the grill over the drip pan. Close the lid and cook for 15 to 20 minutes. Open the lid, rotate the tenderloins 180 degrees, close the lid, and cook for another 10 to 15 minutes. Open the lid and, using an instant-read thermometer, test the internal temperature of the turkey; you are looking for 163°F to 165°F.

5. When the tenderloins are done, remove them from the grill and loosely cover with aluminum foil to rest for 5 to 10 minutes.

6. After resting, transfer the tenderloins to a cutting board. Remove and discard the twine. Cut the tenderloins into 1-inch-thick slices. Place them on a serving plate and spoon any leftover resting juices over the slices.

PULLED CHICKEN ENCHILADAS

SERVES 4 TO 6 / **PREP TIME:** 10 to 15 minutes / **COOK TIME:** 50 minutes to 1 hour
SUGGESTED WOOD: Mesquite lump charcoal

I like using chicken breasts for this recipe and grilling them over high heat for a few minutes, then braising them with green chiles and tomatoes until they are shred-apart tender. These enchiladas can also be made with leftover chicken, pulled pork, or brisket.

4 or 5 chicken boneless, skinless breasts

1 tablespoon Southwestern Seasoning (page 197)

Avocado oil spray

1 (10-ounce) can diced tomatoes with green chiles, such as Rotel, with their juices

8 to 12 white corn tortillas

16 ounces sour cream, divided

8 ounces shredded Monterey Jack cheese, divided

½ cup diced white onion

½ cup chopped cilantro

1. Pat the chicken breasts dry with a paper towel. Butterfly them to create two still-attached halves, cutting them horizontally through the middle and opening them, and sprinkle both sides with the seasoning. Spray both sides with avocado oil and set aside.

2. Set up your grill for indirect cooking (see page 4). Fill a charcoal chimney with mesquite lump charcoal and light it with a fire starter cube. When the coals have turned gray, dump them into the grill on the side opposite the disposable aluminum pan, replace the cooking grate, close the lid, and open the top and bottom vents until the grill temperature registers about 300°F. Continue to monitor the grill, adjusting the vents as needed, until it reaches a cooking temperature of 325°F to 350°F.

3. When the grill is up to temperature, place the chicken breasts directly over the coals on the hot side. Close the lid and cook for 2 to 3 minutes. Open the lid, flip the breasts, and cook for another 2 to 3 minutes with the lid closed. Remove the chicken breasts from the grill and place them in a disposable aluminum pan. Cover the breasts with the diced tomatoes and chiles, then cover the pan with aluminum foil. Place the pan on the indirect side of the grill, close the lid, and cook for 20 to 25 minutes, until the chicken shreds easily.

4. Take the chicken off the grill. Open the foil and shred the chicken into the pan juices. Spray both sides of the tortillas with avocado oil.

5. Spray another disposable aluminum pan with avocado oil, then spread a spoonful or two of sour cream all over the bottom of the pan. To build the enchiladas, place 1 tablespoon of shredded Monterey Jack cheese in the center of a tortilla, then top it with some shredded chicken. Roll the tortilla into a tube shape and place it, seam-side down, in the pan on top of the sour cream. Repeat filling the remaining tortillas as above. Spread the remaining sour cream over the enchiladas. Top with diced white onions and 1 cup of shredded Monterey Jack cheese. Cover the pan with aluminum foil and place on the indirect side of the grill, close the lid, and cook for 15 to 20 minutes. Open the lid, rotate the pan 180 degrees, and remove the foil. Close the lid and cook for another 10 to 15 minutes, until the cheese melts.

6. When the enchiladas are bubbling and the cheese is melted, remove the pan from the grill and let rest for 5 to 10 minutes. Top with chopped cilantro and serve.

PRO TIP: Opening up, or butterflying, the breasts allows you to get more surface area seasoned and the chicken to cook faster.

Salt and Pepper Duck Wings

SERVES 4 TO 6 / **PREP TIME:** 8 hours to overnight / **COOK TIME:** 30 to 45 minutes
SUGGESTED WOOD: Cherrywood chunks

I like serving these duck wings with Classic White BBQ Sauce, but you can use the Southwest Sweet Heat BBQ Sauce (page 199) or the Sticky Honey Teriyaki Sauce (page 198) as well.

12 duck wings, separated into flats and drumettes

1 (16-ounce) bottle Italian dressing

2 to 3 tablespoons SPJG Rub (page 194)

Butter-flavored vegetable oil spray

2 to 3 scallions, sliced

Classic White BBQ Sauce (page 200), to taste

1. Pat the wings dry with a paper towel. With a fork, poke several holes all over each wing and place them in a resealable plastic bag or glass bowl. Add the Italian dressing and toss the wings to coat evenly. Refrigerate for at least 8 hours or overnight.

2. Place a wire rack over a foil-lined baking sheet. Remove the wings from the marinade and discard the marinade. Lay the wings on the wire rack and pat dry with a paper towel. Season with the rub and refrigerate uncovered for 30 to 45 minutes to dry out the skins.

3. Set up your grill for indirect cooking (see page 4). Fill a charcoal chimney with lump charcoal and light it with a fire starter cube. When the coals have turned gray, dump them into the grill on the side opposite the disposable aluminum pan, replace the cooking grate, close the lid, and open the top and bottom vents until the grill temperature registers about 300°F. Continue to monitor the grill, adjusting the vents as needed, until it reaches a cooking temperature of 325°F to 350°F. About 15 minutes before you plan to cook, place 1 or 2 medium cherrywood chunks directly on the hot coals, then close the lid.

4. When the grill is up to temperature, spray the wings with the butter spray, then place them on the indirect side, close the lid, and cook for 15 minutes. Open the lid, spray the wings again, then flip them over, close the lid, and cook for 15 minutes more, or until the wings have an internal temperature of at least 165°F and the skin is golden brown.

5. Remove the wings from the grill and set aside to rest for 5 to 10 minutes.

6. To serve, place the wings on a serving platter and top with sliced scallions. Serve with the white sauce on the side.

PRO TIP: I cook these wings until they have an internal temperature of 185°F to 190°F. I like the skin cooked longer, and the wings will be more tender. Spray with butter-flavored spray while cooking for a nice golden-brown skin.

Al Pastor Chicken Tacos

SERVES 4 TO 6 / **PREP TIME:** 3 to 4 hours / **COOK TIME:** 20 to 25 minutes
SUGGESTED WOOD: Mesquite lump charcoal

Pork is traditionally used for al pastor tacos, but I love using boneless, skinless chicken thighs for this recipe. Make sure to use thighs because they tend to be moister and more flavorful than white meat, which can dry out easily.

6 to 10 boneless, skinless chicken thighs
1 cup pineapple juice
¼ cup white vinegar
¼ cup canola oil
4 or 5 garlic cloves, diced
2 or 3 chipotles in adobo sauce, diced, plus 1 tablespoon adobo sauce
1 tablespoon Southwestern Seasoning (page 197)
1 tablespoon achiote paste
1 cup finely diced white onion, divided
½ cup finely diced pineapple
1 jalapeño, finely diced
1 bunch cilantro, chopped
12 corn tortillas
Avocado oil spray

1. Pat the chicken thighs dry with a paper towel to remove excess moisture and lay them on a cutting board. In a large glass bowl or resealable plastic bag, combine the pineapple juice, white vinegar, canola oil, garlic, chipotles and adobo sauce, seasoning mix, achiote paste, and ½ cup of diced onion and stir to combine thoroughly. (You can also use a food processor to combine the marinade, then pour it into the bowl or resealable bag.) Add the thighs to the marinade, and toss to coat evenly. Refrigerate for 3 to 4 hours.

2. Place a wire rack over a foil-lined baking sheet. Remove the thighs from the marinade and lay them on the rack. Discard the leftover marinade. Pat the thighs dry with paper towels.

3. In a bowl, make a salsa by combining the remaining ½ cup of onion, the diced pineapple, jalapeño, and cilantro. Cover and refrigerate until ready to use.

4. Set up your grill for direct cooking (see page 3). Fill a charcoal chimney with mesquite lump charcoal and light it with a fire starter cube. When the coals have turned gray, dump them into the grill grate or basket in an even layer, close the lid, replace the cooking grate, and open the top and bottom vents. You are looking for the grill thermometer to be at least 450°F (this will take 20 to 30 minutes).

5. When the grill is ready, open the lid and place the thighs evenly around the grill, then close the lid and cook for 8 to 10 minutes. Open the lid, flip them over, close the lid, and cook for another 8 to 10 minutes. Open the lid and, using an instant-read thermometer, test the thighs for doneness (163°F to 165°F). Continue to cook and rotate until the temperature is reached.

6. When done, remove the thighs from the grill and place them on a plate, loosely covered with aluminum foil, to rest for 5 to 10 minutes. While the thighs are resting, spray the tortillas with avocado oil and place them on the grill for 30 seconds to 1 minute per side to heat through. Remove and set aside.

7. Place the thighs on a cutting board and cut them into ½-inch cubes. Place the chicken back on the resting plate and toss with any leftover juices.

8. To serve, fill a tortilla with chicken and top with the onion-pineapple salsa. Enjoy!

Chapter 6

SEAFOOD

◀ Hot Smoked Cedar-Plank
Salmon (page 136)

Hot Smoked Cedar-Plank Salmon

SERVES 4 TO 6 / PREP TIME: 20 to 30 minutes / **COOK TIME:** 25 to 30 minutes
SUGGESTED WOOD: Cedarwood plank

I was invited to teach and cook at a barbecue competition on the Gold Coast of Australia, so I cooked this salmon recipe, along with the Garlic Butter Lobster Tail Skewers on page 140, and tied for first place.

1 (4- to 6-pound) salmon fillet, skin removed

1½ tablespoons Poultry and Seafood Rub (page 196)

8 ounces cream cheese, softened

¼ cup mayonnaise

¼ cup chopped fresh dill

Juice of 1 lemon

1 teaspoon hot sauce, preferably Cholula

1 cup crumbled Ritz crackers

3 tablespoons salted butter, melted

¼ cup chopped fresh chives

1. Soak a cedar plank in water for 20 minutes. Pat the salmon dry with a paper towel and lay it on a cutting board. Cut the salmon into 4 to 6 equal portions. Sprinkle all sides with the rub.

2. In a bowl, combine the cream cheese, mayonnaise, dill, lemon juice, and hot sauce and blend well. Cover and refrigerate until needed. In a separate bowl, stir together the crumbled crackers and melted butter and set aside.

3. Remove the cedar plank from the water, then lay the salmon portions across it, leaving room in between each piece. Top each piece with equal amounts of the cream cheese mixture, then top with equal amounts of the cracker topping. Cover and refrigerate until you're ready to grill.

4. Set up your grill for indirect cooking (see page 4). Fill a charcoal chimney with lump charcoal and light it with a fire starter cube. When the coals have turned gray, dump them into the grill on the side opposite the disposable aluminum pan, replace the cooking grate, close the lid, and open the top and bottom vents until the grill temperature registers about 300°F. Continue to monitor the grill, adjusting the vents as needed, until it reaches a cooking temperature of 325°F to 350°F.

5. When the grill is up to temperature, open the lid and place the cedar-planked salmon on the direct heat side over the coals. Close the lid and cook for 10 to 15 minutes. Open the lid and move the cedar plank and salmon to the indirect side of the grill. Close the lid and cook for 10 minutes more. Open the lid and test the internal temperature of the salmon. You're looking for an internal temperature of 120°F to 145°F; I like my salmon around 130°F.

6. When the salmon is done to your preference, remove the cedar plank and salmon from the grill and let it rest for 5 to 10 minutes.

7. To serve, place the cedar plank on a plate in the center of the table, top the salmon with the chives, and enjoy!

PRO TIP: Make sure to keep an eye on the cedar plank. You want it to smolder a bit so the fish can pick up some smoke flavor, but you do not want it to burn. Check on it every 5 minutes or so with a quick peek under the lid. If it starts to burn, move it to the indirect side of the grill.

SOUTHWESTERN CRAB CAKES

MAKES 6 CRAB CAKES / **PREP TIME:** 30 to 45 minutes / **COOK TIME:** 10 to 15 minutes
SUGGESTED WOOD: Applewood chips

These are not your typical crab cakes. I made them for a video shoot and added a Southwestern twist, and they were a huge hit. The crunchy tortilla chips add great texture to the creamy crab mixture.

1 pound jumbo lump
   crabmeat
1 jalapeño, diced
1 bunch cilantro,
   chopped, divided
½ cup mayonnaise
½ cup Mexican crema
Juice of 1 lemon
½ cup crushed tortilla
   chips, plus extra
   for coating
1 large egg, beaten
1 tablespoon Poultry and
   Seafood Rub (page 196)
Avocado oil spray
   or 2 tablespoons
   salted butter
Lemon wedges,
   for serving

1. In a large bowl, combine the crabmeat, jalapeño, three-quarters of the chopped cilantro, the mayonnaise, crema, lemon juice, tortilla chips, beaten egg, and the rub and mix thoroughly. Form 6 even-size cakes from the mixture. Place a layer of crushed tortilla chips on a plate and lightly press each cake into the crushed chips to create a nice crust. Set aside.

2. Set up your grill for direct cooking (see page 3). Fill a charcoal chimney with charcoal and light it with a fire starter cube. When the coals have turned gray, dump them into the grill grate or basket in an even layer, close the lid, and open the top and bottom vents. For this recipe I like to use either flat-top grill grates or a cast-iron pan set on the cooking grate over the fire to get a good sear on the crab cakes. I preheat the grates or pan on the grill for 15 minutes before cooking. Spray the grates with avocado oil before using them or, if you're using a cast-iron pan, melt the butter in the pan.

3. Right before you plan to cook, scatter a small handful of applewood chips directly on the hot coals.

4. Open the lid, place the crab cakes on the preheated flat-top or cast-iron pan, and cook for 4 to 5 minutes, until the outside turns golden brown. Carefully flip the crab cakes and cook for another 4 to 5 minutes, until the other side is golden brown.

5. When the cakes are done, remove them from the flat top or pan and set aside.

6. To serve, place the crab cakes on a platter and top with the remaining chopped cilantro with lemon wedges on the side.

PRO TIP: I like to use the avocado crema from the Skirt Steak Carne Asada Tacos recipe (page 54) on the crab cakes as a topping or on the side for dipping.

Garlic Butter Lobster Tail Skewers

SERVES 4 TO 6 / PREP TIME: 30 to 45 minutes / **COOK TIME:** 8 to 10 minutes
SUGGESTED WOOD: Applewood chips

I paired these tasty skewers with the Hot Smoked Cedar-Plank Salmon (page 136) at a barbecue competition on the Australian Gold Coast, and they tied for first place. This versatile dish can be served as an appetizer or a main dish.

4 to 6 lobster tails
Juice of 1 lemon, divided
1¼ tablespoons Poultry
   and Seafood Rub
   (page 196)
1 cup (2 sticks) salted
   butter, melted
5 or 6 garlic
   cloves, minced
4 to 6 thyme sprigs
Smoked Garlic Aioli
   (page 203), for serving
Lemon wedges,
   for serving

1. With a pair of kitchen shears, cut down the center back of each tail to open up the shell. Remove the meat in one piece and lay it out on a cutting board. Skewer each tail on a wood or metal skewer. (If using wooden skewers, soak them in water for 10 to 20 minutes so they don't burn while cooking.) Squeeze half the lemon juice over the skewers and season both sides with the rub. Place them in the refrigerator while you ready your grill.

2. Set up your grill for indirect cooking (see page 4). Fill a charcoal chimney with lump charcoal and light it with a fire starter cube. When the coals have turned gray, dump them into the grill on the side opposite the disposable aluminum pan, replace the cooking grate, close the lid, and open the top and bottom vents until the grill temperature registers about 300°F. Continue to monitor the grill, adjusting the vents as needed, until it reaches a cooking temperature of 325°F to 350°F.

3. In a small disposable aluminum loaf pan, combine the butter, the remaining lemon juice, the garlic, and thyme. Place the pan on the indirect side of the grill to warm through for 10 to 15 minutes, until the butter

melts. Remove the skewers from the refrigerator and brush them with the melted butter. Scatter a small handful of applewood chips over the coals and place the skewers directly on the hot side of the grill over the coals. Cook for 1 to 2 minutes, brush them with butter, then flip them over and brush again. Cook for another 1 to 2 minutes, brush them with butter, then flip again. Continue to flip and baste with butter until the internal temperature of the lobster is about 135°F. If any lobster tails are cooking too quickly, or are done before the others, move to the side with indirect heat.

4. The lobster tails are done when they turn white and are no longer gray. Remove them from the grill and baste them again with the butter. Let rest for 5 to 10 minutes.

5. Serve the skewers individually with aioli and lemon wedges on the side. Cheers!

Bacon-Wrapped Scallops with Cilantro Jalapeño Butter

SERVES 4 TO 6 / PREP TIME: 45 minutes to 1 hour / COOK TIME: 15 to 20 minutes
SUGGESTED WOOD: Cherrywood chunk

When shopping for scallops, I like to buy the biggest ones I can find. Diver scallops tend to be the largest, as they are harvested by divers instead of by dredging the ocean floor, and the divers tend to pick the largest ones they can find. Make sure the bacon is as thin as possible to avoid overcooking the scallops.

8 tablespoons (1 stick) salted butter, softened

½ cup chopped fresh cilantro

1 jalapeño, finely diced

Juice of 1 lime, plus extra lime wedges for serving

10 to 12 large scallops, preferably diver scallops

1½ tablespoons Southwestern Seasoning (page 197)

1 (12-ounce) package thin-cut bacon

1. In a bowl, combine the softened butter, cilantro, jalapeño, and lime juice and stir to combine thoroughly. Spoon the butter onto a piece of plastic wrap and form it into a log shape by rolling it in the plastic and sealing the ends. Refrigerate to firm it up before use.

2. Lay the scallops on a cutting board and pat them dry with paper towels. Sprinkle both sides with the seasoning and set them aside.

3. Cut the bacon strips in half lengthwise. Lay a scallop, flat-side down, in the middle of one half of a piece of bacon and fold the bacon over on both sides of the scallop. Cut the bacon with a knife or scissors until you have about ½ to 1 inch of overlap on the two ends. Flip the scallop over, rotate it 90 degrees, and lay it seam-side down on the other half piece of bacon, in a plus-sign shape. Fold the bacon over the scallop and cut it so you have a 1-inch overlap. Make sure the bacon is tight around the scallop. Repeat with the remaining scallops and bacon, place them seam-side down on a plate, cover, and refrigerate until ready to cook.

4. Set up your grill for indirect cooking (see page 4). Fill a charcoal chimney with lump charcoal and light it with a fire starter cube. When the coals have turned gray, dump them into the grill on the side opposite the disposable aluminum pan, replace the cooking grate, close the lid, and open the top and bottom vents until the grill temperature registers about 275°F. Continue to monitor the grill, adjusting the vents as needed, until it reaches a cooking temperature of 300°F to 325°F. About 15 minutes before you plan to cook, place 1 small chunk of cherrywood on the coals, then close the lid.

5. When the grill is ready and the smoke is clean, remove both the butter and scallops from the refrigerator. Slice the butter into the same number of disks as scallops and place one on top of each scallop. Open the grill lid and place each butter-topped scallop seam-side down on the indirect side of the grill. Close the lid and cook for 8 to 10 minutes. Open the lid and rotate the scallops 180 degrees, close the lid, and cook for another 8 to 10 minutes. Open the lid and check the internal temperature of the scallop with an instant-read thermometer. You are looking for an internal temperature of 125°F to 130°F and for the bacon to be cooked.

6. When the scallops are done, remove them from the grill and let rest for 5 to 10 minutes. Serve with lime wedges on the side.

PRO TIP: I like to move the scallops directly over the coals for the last 1 to 2 minutes of cooking to crisp up the bacon a little more. Serve these on top of Elote Salad (page 166) for an awesome presentation and meal.

MESQUITE GRILLED SHRIMP AND AVOCADO SALAD

SERVES 4 TO 6 / **PREP TIME:** 30 minutes / **COOK TIME:** 20 minutes
SUGGESTED WOOD: Mesquite lump charcoal

I was a contestant on the Discovery Channel's *Smoked* series, and shrimp was one of the mystery items we were given to cook. I whipped up this recipe for the judges, and they were so impressed that they awarded me the win!

1 ear of corn, husk and silk removed

Avocado oil spray

1½ tablespoons Poultry and Seafood Rub (page 196)

18 large raw shrimp, peeled and deveined

3 avocados

¼ cup diced red onion

1 Roma tomato, cored, seeded, and diced

1 jalapeño, diced

2 cups shredded green cabbage

¼ cup chopped fresh cilantro, plus extra for garnish

2 limes

Salt

Freshly ground black pepper

½ teaspoon toasted sesame oil

1. Set up your grill for direct cooking (see page 3) by filling a charcoal chimney with mesquite lump charcoal and lighting it with a fire starter cube. When the coals have turned gray, dump them into the grill and adjust the vents to fully open.

2. Spray the ear of corn with avocado oil and lightly sprinkle it with the rub. When the grill is ready and there is little to no smoke coming from the vents, place the corn on the grill and cook, rotating it occasionally, for 8 to 10 minutes, until the corn has caramelized and turned golden brown. Remove the corn and set aside.

3. Skewer 4 or 5 shrimp on a wooden skewer, leaving space between each shrimp. Sprinkle both sides with the rub and spray with avocado oil. Repeat with the remaining shrimp, then place the skewers over direct heat and cook for 1 to 2 minutes per side; the shrimp are done when they turn pink. Remove the shrimp from the grill and set aside.

4. Halve the avocados and remove the pits. Scoop out the avocado into a bowl, reserving the empty skins. Mash the avocado with a fork into a smooth yet chunky texture. Add the onion, tomatoes, jalapeños, cabbage, and cilantro, then stir to combine.

5. Slice the corn kernels off the cob and add them to the avocado mixture, squeeze the juice of 1 lime into the mixture, and season with salt and pepper to taste. Drizzle the sesame oil over the mixture and stir to combine.

6. Divide the avocado mixture evenly among the avocado shell halves and top each with 3 shrimp. Garnish with cilantro and cut the remaining lime into wedges for serving.

PRO TIP: Soak the wooden skewers in water for 30 minutes before using so they don't burn on the grill.

Crawfish Étouffée Skewers with Onion, Bell Peppers, and Cayenne Butter

SERVES 4 TO 6 / **PREP TIME:** 20 to 30 minutes / **COOK TIME:** 5 to 10 minutes
SUGGESTED WOOD: Pecan wood chips

These crawfish étouffée skewers take me back to the time I lived in southern Mississippi as a kid. One of my favorite times of year was crawfish season and my mom's crawfish étouffée. The smell throughout the house while she was cooking was amazing. This is my take on her recipe using a grill instead of the range.

2 large sweet onions, cut into bite-size pieces

2 to 3 pounds fresh raw crawfish tails, shelled

1 large green bell pepper, cut into bite-size pieces

1 large red bell pepper, cut into bite-size pieces

2 tablespoons Poultry and Seafood Rub (page 196)

1 cup (2 sticks) salted butter, softened

1 shallot, diced

5 or 6 garlic cloves, minced

1 tablespoon cayenne pepper

1 tablespoon Old Bay Seasoning

Steamed rice, for serving

1. On a presoaked wood or metal skewer, thread a piece of onion, then a crawfish tail, then a green and red bell pepper piece, repeating the process until the skewer is full. Thread the remaining ingredients on skewers and refrigerate them all until you're ready to cook.

2. In a small disposable aluminum loaf pan, combine the rub, butter, shallot, garlic, cayenne, and Old Bay and blend them thoroughly.

3. Set up your grill for direct cooking (see page 3). Fill a charcoal chimney full of charcoal and light it with a fire starter cube. When the coals have turned gray, dump them into the grill grate or basket in an even layer, replace the cooking grate, close the lid, and open the top and bottom vents. You are looking for the grill thermometer to be at least 450°F (this takes 20 to 30 minutes).

4. When the grill is up to temperature, place the butter mixture on the grill, close the lid, and cook for 5 to 10 minutes, until the butter is melted, then move it to the side of the grill. Scatter a handful of pecan wood chips directly over the coals, then place the skewers evenly around the grill and brush them with the butter. Close the lid and cook for 1 to 2 minutes. Open the lid, brush the skewers with more butter, and give them a flip. Brush again with butter and cook for another 1 to 2 minutes, leaving the grill lid open if you're using a charcoal grill. Baste the tails with butter throughout the cook time. When the crawfish tails are no longer gray but a pinkish-red color, they are done.

5. Remove the skewers and let rest on a plate for 5 to 10 minutes.

6. To serve, place the skewers over a bed of rice and drizzle any reserved butter over them.

> **PRO TIP:** These skewers will cook quickly, so make sure to keep them buttered and continue to rotate them throughout the cook time to avoid overcooking.

Ahi Tuna Sliders with Wasabi Broccoli Slaw

SERVES 4 TO 6 / **PREP TIME:** 2 to 3 hours / **COOK TIME:** 10 to 15 minutes
SUGGESTED WOOD: Cherrywood chips

I like to use GrillGrates for this recipe (and many other grilled fish recipes). You can use them to get grill marks or, with the flat top, for a good sear on the fish. They also help prevent food from falling through the cooking grates when flipping or removing it from the grill.

8 to 12 (1½-inch-thick) sushi-grade ahi tuna steaks
½ cup soy sauce
¼ cup ponzu
1 tablespoon sriracha
1 teaspoon toasted sesame oil
1 teaspoon ground ginger or grated fresh ginger
1 (16-ounce) bag shredded broccoli
½ cup mayonnaise
1½ teaspoons wasabi paste, plus more to taste
1 (12-pack) sesame seed slider buns
Avocado oil spray

1. Cut the tuna steaks down to roughly the size of the slider buns and pat them dry with a paper towel.

2. In a glass bowl or large resealable plastic bag, combine the soy sauce, ponzu, sriracha, sesame oil, and ginger. Add the tuna steaks to the marinade, mix to cover thoroughly, and refrigerate for 2 to 3 hours.

3. In a bowl, combine the shredded broccoli, mayonnaise, and wasabi paste. Taste and add more wasabi paste if you like more kick. Cover and refrigerate until ready to serve.

4. Set up your grill for direct cooking (see page 3). Fill a charcoal chimney with charcoal and light it with a fire starter cube. When the coals have turned gray, dump them into the grill grate or basket in an even layer, replace the cooking grate, add GrillGrates (if using) to the grill, close the lid, and open the top and bottom vents. You are looking for the grill thermometer to be at least 450°F (it will take 20 to 30 minutes).

5. Remove the tuna steaks from the marinade and discard any excess marinade. Open the grill lid and scatter a small handful of cherrywood chips around the coals. Spray the grates with avocado oil, then place the tuna on the grill grates. Close the lid and cook for 1 minute. Open the lid and give the steaks a 90-degree turn. Close the lid and cook for 1 minute. After 1 minute, open the lid, spray the steaks with avocado oil, and carefully flip them. Close the lid and cook for 1 minute more. Open the lid and, using an instant-read thermometer, test the internal temperature. I like mine medium-rare to medium, or an internal temperature of 120°F to 125°F.

6. When the steaks are to your desired doneness, remove them from the grill and let rest for 5 minutes. While the steaks are resting, toast the slider buns on the GrillGrates for a minute or two until they get a nice char on the inside but are not burnt.

7. To serve, place a tuna steak on the bottom bun, top it with a spoonful of broccoli slaw, add the top bun, and dig in!

SALMON-STUFFED BACON-WRAPPED JUMBO PRAWNS

SERVES 4 TO 6 / PREP TIME: 45 minutes to 1 hour / **COOK TIME:** 25 to 30 minutes
SUGGESTED WOOD: Cherrywood chunks

This recipe is inspired by my good friend and chef Christina Fitzgerald. She made her lobster-filled, bacon-wrapped shrimp and won the seafood category at the Memphis in May World Championship Barbecue Cooking Contest. This is my version using smoked salmon and cream cheese as the filling.

8 to 12 raw jumbo shrimp, peeled and deveined, tails on

8 ounces smoked salmon, shredded

½ cup cream cheese, softened

¼ cup mayonnaise

¼ cup chopped fresh chives

1 jalapeño, finely diced

1 (12-ounce) package thin-sliced bacon

Sweet Heat BBQ Sauce (page 199), to taste

1. Butterfly the shrimp to prepare them for filling, cutting them horizontally through the middle but making sure not to cut all the way through. In a bowl, make the filling by combining the smoked salmon, cream cheese, mayonnaise, chives, and jalapeño and mixing thoroughly.

2. Spoon approximately 1 heaping tablespoon of the filling onto each butterflied shrimp and close the shrimp around the filling. Wrap a piece of bacon tightly around the shrimp, starting at the non-tail end and leaving the tail exposed. Secure the bacon with a toothpick. Repeat with the remaining shrimp and filling. Place them in the refrigerator until you're ready to cook.

3. Set up your grill for indirect cooking (see page 4). Fill a charcoal chimney with lump charcoal and light it with a fire starter cube. When the coals have turned gray, dump them into the grill on the side opposite the disposable aluminum pan, replace the cooking grate, close the lid, and open the top and bottom vents until the grill temperature registers about 275°F. Continue to monitor the grill, adjusting the vents as needed, until it reaches a cooking temperature of 300°F to 325°F. About 15 minutes before you plan to cook, place 1 or 2 small chunks of cherrywood on the coals, then close the lid.

4. When the grill is hot and the smoke is clean, open the lid and place the shrimp on the indirect side of the grill over the drip pan. Close the lid and cook for 10 minutes. Open the lid and give the shrimp a flip, close the lid, and cook for another 10 minutes, or until the bacon is cooked. The shrimp will be pinkish-white and no longer gray when they're done.

5. Remove the shrimp from the grill, brush them with the barbecue sauce and place them back on the grill, this time directly over the coals, for 1 minute to set the sauce. Remove the shrimp from the grill and set aside to rest for 5 minutes.

6. Make sure to remove the toothpicks before serving.

PRO TIP: I like to serve these with the citrus mayo from the Bacon-Wrapped Asparagus (page 189).

Crusted Catfish Po' Boy with Smoked Garlic Aioli

SERVES 4 TO 6 / **PREP TIME:** 30 to 45 minutes / **COOK TIME:** 20 to 25 minutes
SUGGESTED WOOD: Pecan wood chips

When I lived in southern Mississippi, we would often visit this little seafood shack, and po' boy sandwiches were the favorite menu item. Crunchy catfish, shrimp, and oysters were the go-to fillings for these. Make sure to load them up with fish, lots of mayonnaise, thinly sliced tomatoes, and shredded lettuce. Don't forget the hot sauce!

4 to 6 boneless, skinless catfish fillets
½ cup mayonnaise
1 tablespoon hot sauce
¾ cup cornmeal
¼ cup all-purpose flour
2 tablespoons Poultry and Seafood Rub (page 196)
Avocado oil spray
1 recipe Smoked Garlic Aioli (page 203)
1 to 2 loaves soft French bread, halved horizontally through the middle
1 head iceberg lettuce, shredded
2 to 3 Roma tomatoes, thinly sliced

1. Lay the catfish on a cutting board and pat it dry with a paper towel.

2. In a small bowl, stir together the mayonnaise and hot sauce and set aside. In a resealable plastic bag, combine the cornmeal, flour, and rub. Shake to combine, then set aside.

3. Lightly brush the fillets with the mayonnaise mixture, then top with a spoonful of the cornmeal mixture, and lightly pat the cornmeal into the fish. Flip the fillets over and repeat until all the fillets are coated. Refrigerate the fillets until you're ready to cook.

4. Set up your grill for direct cooking (see page 3). Fill a charcoal chimney with charcoal and light it with a fire starter cube. When the coals have turned gray, dump them into the grill grate or basket in an even layer, replace the cooking grate, add Grill Grates (if using) flat-side up to the grill, close the lid, and open the top and bottom vents. You are looking for the grill temperature to be at least 450°F (this will take 20 to 30 minutes).

5. When the grill is hot and ready, remove the catfish from the refrigerator and spray both sides with avocado oil. Open the grill lid and spray the flat-top grates with the avocado oil. Scatter a small handful of pecan wood chips around the coals, then place the fillets on the flat-top grates. Close the lid and cook for 8 to 10 minutes. Open the lid and check the bottom of the fillets. When they are golden brown, spray the tops again with avocado oil and, using a long spatula, flip them. Close the lid and cook for another 8 to 10 minutes, until golden brown. When the fish starts to look flaky, remove the fillets from the grill to a paper towel–lined plate and let rest.

6. Slather aioli on both sides of the French bread halves. Place the catfish fillets on the bottom and top with shredded lettuce and sliced tomatoes. Slice the French bread loaves into serving sizes.

CEDAR-PLANK LEMON-PEPPER SALMON

SERVES 4 TO 6 / **PREP TIME:** 15 to 20 minutes / **COOK TIME:** 25 to 30 minutes
SUGGESTED WOOD: Cedarwood plank

This dish is an awesome centerpiece for a whole salmon fillet dinner, or it can be an appealing appetizer. To serve it as an appetizer, place it on the table and add crackers all around the salmon and a few forks for digging in.

1 (5- to 6-pound) salmon
    fillet, skin on
1 tablespoon grated
    lemon zest
Juice of 2 lemons
½ cup mayonnaise
1 tablespoon freshly
    ground black pepper
1 lemon, thinly sliced
1 tablespoon Poultry and
    Seafood Rub (page 196)

1. Soak a cedar plank in water for 20 minutes. Lay the salmon on a cutting board and pat it dry with a paper towel. In a bowl, combine the lemon zest and juice, mayonnaise, and pepper and blend well.

2. Remove the cedar plank from water, then lay the lemon slices on the entire plank in an even layer. Place the salmon fillet on top of the lemon slices. Brush the salmon with half the lemon-pepper mayonnaise, then sprinkle it lightly with the rub. Refrigerate until the grill is ready.

3. Set up your grill for indirect cooking (see page 4). Fill a charcoal chimney with lump charcoal and light it with a fire starter cube. When the coals have turned gray, dump them into the grill on the side opposite the disposable aluminum pan, replace the cooking grate, close the lid, and open the top and bottom vents until the grill temperature registers about 300°F. Continue to monitor the grill, adjusting the vents as needed, until it reaches a cooking temperature of 325°F to 350°F.

4. When the grill is up to temperature, open the lid and place the cedar-planked salmon on the direct-heat side over the coals. Close the lid and cook for 10 to 15 minutes. Open the lid and move the cedar plank to the indirect side of the grill and brush the salmon with the remaining lemon-pepper mayonnaise. Close the lid and cook for 10 minutes. Open the lid and test for doneness. You are looking for an internal temperature between 120°F and 145°F; I like my salmon around 130°F.

5. When the salmon is cooked to your desired doneness, remove the cedar plank and salmon from the grill. Let rest for 5 to 10 minutes before serving.

PRO TIP: I like to make extra lemon-pepper mayonnaise and drizzle some over the salmon when serving or serve it on the side.

Hot and Spicy Grilled Oysters on the Half Shell

SERVES 4 TO 6 / **PREP TIME:** 20 to 30 minutes / **COOK TIME:** 10 to 12 minutes
SUGGESTED WOOD: Mesquite lump charcoal

If you like oysters, you are going to love this recipe. Cooking them hot and fast over mesquite wood adds a nice smoky flavor. I buy them pre-shucked, but the key is to have them as fresh as possible and keep them cold until you are ready to cook.

18 to 20 large oysters on the half shell
Hot sauce, to taste
Juice of 1 lemon
5 or 6 garlic cloves, minced
2 or 3 jalapeños, sliced
Crumbled cotija cheese
1 bunch cilantro, chopped
Lime wedges, for serving

1. Set up your grill for direct cooking (see page 3). Fill a charcoal chimney with mesquite lump charcoal and light it with a fire starter cube. When the coals have turned gray, dump them into the grill grate or basket in an even layer, replace the cooking grate, close the lid, and open the top and bottom vents. You are looking for the grill temperature to be at least 450°F (this will take 20 to 30 minutes).

2. Place a wire rack over a foil-lined baking sheet. Lay the oysters in the grooves of the rack so the liquid does not run out of the shell. Add a dash of hot sauce to each oyster and sprinkle the lemon juice over all of them. Top each one with a pinch of minced garlic and a jalapeño slice.

3. When the grill is up to temperature, open the lid and place the wire rack and oysters directly on the grill. Close the lid and cook for 10 to 12 minutes, then remove the rack and place it back on the foil-lined baking sheet, making sure to keep as much liquid in the shells as possible.

4. Sprinkle crumbled cotija cheese and chopped cilantro over each oyster. Serve with some *cervezas* and lime wedges, and enjoy!

Garlic and Thyme Butter Braised Shrimp

SERVES 4 TO 6 / **PREP TIME:** 30 to 45 minutes / **COOK TIME:** 10 to 20 minutes
SUGGESTED WOOD: Applewood chunks

When it comes to shrimp, the bigger the better for this recipe. I like to get the freshest and largest I can find, so they have time to cook and accept some light applewood-smoke flavor. They will turn from a grayish color to pinkish-white and form a C shape when cooked. Shrimp can have a rubbery texture when overdone; when they form an O, they have cooked too long.

2 to 3 pounds large
  shrimp, deveined,
  shell on
1 cup (2 sticks)
  salted butter
6 to 8 thyme sprigs
5 or 6 garlic
  cloves, minced
2 teaspoon red
  pepper flakes
1 teaspoon Poultry and
  Seafood Rub (page 196)
½ cup shredded
  Parmesan cheese
1 baguette, cut into
  1-inch-thick slices
Avocado oil spray
¼ cup chopped
  fresh parsley

1. Set up your grill for indirect cooking (see page 4). Fill a charcoal chimney with lump charcoal and light it with a fire starter cube. When the coals have turned gray, dump them into the grill on the side opposite the disposable aluminum pan, replace the cooking grate, close the lid, and open the top and bottom vents until the grill temperature registers about 300°F. Continue to monitor the grill, adjusting the vents as needed, until it reaches a cooking temperature of 325°F to 350°F. About 15 minutes before you plan to cook, place 1 or 2 applewood chunks on the hot coals, then close the lid.

2. In a disposable aluminum half pan, combine the butter, thyme, garlic, red pepper flakes, and the rub. Place the pan on the indirect side of the grill, close the lid, and cook for 5 to 10 minutes, until the butter melts, then remove the pan. Place the shrimp in the pan and toss to coat them evenly in the butter. Place the pan back on the indirect side of the grill, close the lid, and cook for 5 to 10 minutes. Open the lid and rotate the pan, toss the shrimp around, and close the lid. Cook for another 5 to 10 minutes. The shrimp are done when they start to turn pinkish and curl into a C shape.

CONTINUED

3. Remove the shrimp from the grill, sprinkle with the Parmesan cheese, and set aside.

4. Spray both sides of the baguette slices with avocado oil. Place them on the hot side of grill, directly over the coals, to toast for 1 to 2 minutes, then flip and toast the other side, being careful not to burn the bread.

5. To serve, transfer the shrimp to a serving plate or bowl and top with chopped parsley. Serve with toasted baguette slices.

MESQUITE GRILLED WHOLE RAINBOW TROUT

SERVES 4 TO 6 / **PREP TIME:** 30 to 45 minutes / **COOK TIME:** 15 to 20 minutes
SUGGESTED WOOD: Mesquite lump charcoal

Cooking a whole fish is easy, and there is a somewhat primal feeling when cooking it over fire. I love cooking rainbow trout hot and fast over mesquite wood. This recipe is easily adaptable to other types of whole fish as well.

2 to 3 whole rainbow
  trout, cleaned
  and gutted
Juice of 2 lemons
3 to 4 tablespoons
  Poultry and Seafood
  Rub (page 196)
2 lemons, thinly sliced
12 dill sprigs
Avocado oil spray
Classic White BBQ Sauce
  (page 200), warmed,
  to taste
¼ cup sliced scallions

1. Place the trout on a cutting board and, using a sharp knife, make three ½-inch-deep slits along the fillet on both sides. Sprinkle the lemon juice over both sides and inside the cavity of the trout. Season the cavity and the entire skin sides with the rub. Place 3 or 4 lemon slices and 3 or 4 dill sprigs in the cavity of each trout. Close the belly of the trout with two or three toothpicks, then refrigerate it while you prepare the grill.

2. Set up your grill for direct cooking (see page 3). Fill a charcoal chimney with mesquite lump charcoal and light it with a fire starter cube. When the coals have turned gray, dump them into the grill grate or basket in an even layer, replace the cooking grate, add GrillGrates (if using), flat-side up, to the grill, close the lid, and open the top and bottom vents. You are looking for the grill temperature to be at least 450°F (this will take 20 to 30 minutes).

CONTINUED

3. When the grill is hot, remove the trout from the refrigerator and spray it with avocado oil. Place the trout on the GrillGrates. Close the lid and cook for 8 to 10 minutes. Open the lid, spray the trout with avocado oil, and flip the trout to cook the other side. Close the lid and cook for another 8 to 10 minutes. Open the lid and, using an instant-read thermometer, check the fish for doneness (at least 145°F). You also want the skin to peel off cleanly and the flesh to start to flake. When the fish is done, carefully remove it from the grill, using a long spatula or tongs to keep it together. Remove the toothpicks and let it rest for 5 to 10 minutes.

4. To serve place the whole trout on a serving platter, drizzle the white sauce all over the fillets, and top with sliced scallions.

Chapter 7

VEGGIES AND SIDES

◀ Bacon-Wrapped Asparagus (page 189)

Garlic Parmesan Balsamic Mushrooms

SERVES 4 TO 6 / **PREP TIME:** 30 to 45 minutes / **COOK TIME:** 15 to 25 minutes
SUGGESTED WOOD: Applewood chunk

I like to cook these mushrooms in a disposable aluminum pie pan. I look for mushrooms that are uniform in size for even cooking.

12 to 18 whole portobello
　mushrooms, 1½ inches
　in diameter, cleaned
Avocado oil spray
8 tablespoons (1 stick)
　salted butter
6 to 8 garlic
　cloves, minced
1¼ tablespoons SPGJ Rub
　(page 194)
½ cup shredded
　Parmesan cheese
Balsamic glaze, for
　drizzling
¼ cup chopped fresh
　parsley, for garnish

1. Cut the end of the stem off each mushroom so they stand upright. Spray a disposable pie pan with avocado oil and place the mushrooms cap-side down in the pan. Cut the butter into ¼-inch slices and place one in the cap of each mushroom. Top each pat of butter with a pinch of minced garlic, then sprinkle the top of each with the rub and set aside.

2. Set up your grill for indirect cooking (see page 4). Fill a charcoal chimney with lump charcoal and light it with a fire starter cube. When the coals have turned gray, dump them into the grill on the side opposite the disposable aluminum pan, replace the cooking grate, close the lid, and open the top and bottom vents until the grill temperature registers about 300°F. Continue to monitor the grill, adjusting the vents as needed, until it reaches a cooking temperature of 325°F to 350°F. About 15 minutes before you plan to cook, place an applewood chunk on the hot coals, then close the lid.

3. When the grill is hot, open the lid and place the pan with the mushrooms on the indirect side of the grill. Close the lid and cook for 10 to 15 minutes. Open the lid, rotate the pan 180 degrees, and evenly divide and sprinkle the Parmesan cheese on the top of each mushroom. Close the lid and cook for another 5 to 10 minutes, until the cheese is melted and the mushrooms are tender; stick a toothpick or wooden skewer into a mushroom to test for tenderness. You are looking for it to slide into the mushroom with very little resistance.

4. When the cheese is melted and the mushrooms are tender, remove the pan from the grill and set it aside. Before serving, drizzle the balsamic glaze over the mushrooms and top with chopped parsley.

ELOTE SALAD

SERVES 4 TO 6 / PREP TIME: 30 to 45 minutes / **COOK TIME:** 10 to 20 minutes
SUGGESTED WOOD: Mesquite wood chips

Elote, or grilled corn with crumbled Mexican cheese, is a typical Southwestern treat. Sweet corn on the cob is grilled and charred over hot mesquite wood, then coated with mayonnaise or crema, crumbled cotija cheese, and Southwestern spices. Typically, it is served on the cob on a wooden skewer and topped with chopped cilantro. This is my version for an "off the cob" elote salad.

6 to 8 ears of corn, husks and silk removed

Avocado oil spray

2 tablespoons Southwestern Seasoning (page 197), divided

1 cup crumbled cotija cheese

½ cup mayonnaise

¼ cup Mexican crema

½ cup diced red onion

½ cup plus 2 tablespoons chopped fresh cilantro, divided

2 serrano peppers, diced

Juice of 1 lime, plus lime wedges for serving

1. Spray the ears of corn with avocado oil and lightly sprinkle them with the seasoning mix, reserving 1 tablespoon of seasoning. Set aside.

2. Set up your grill for indirect cooking (see page 4). Fill a charcoal chimney with lump charcoal and light it with a fire starter cube. When the coals have turned gray, dump them into the grill on the side opposite the disposable aluminum pan, replace the cooking grate, close the lid, and open the top and bottom vents until the grill temperature registers about 325°F. Continue to monitor the grill, adjusting the vents as needed, until it reaches a cooking temperature of 350°F to 375°F.

3. When the grill is hot, open the lid and scatter a handful of mesquite wood chips on the hot coals, then place the ears of corn evenly around the grill on the direct heat side. Close the lid and cook for 5 to 10 minutes. Open the lid, give the ears a 180-degree roll, close the lid, and cook for 5 to 10 minutes more. You want the corn to char a bit and caramelize but not burn. If it looks like it is getting too dark, move it to the indirect-heat side.

4. When the corn is done, remove it from the grill and let it rest for 5 to 10 minutes, then slice the corn kernels off the cob and place them in a large bowl. Add the cotija cheese, mayonnaise, crema, red onion, ½ cup of cilantro, the serrano peppers, lime juice, and the reserved 1 tablespoon of seasoning. Stir to combine thoroughly.

5. Top the salad with the remaining 2 tablespoons of cilantro and serve with lime wedges.

PRO TIP: For a more traditional version, leave the corn on the cob, then coat with the mayonnaise, cotija cheese, seasoning, and cilantro.

Bacon-Wrapped Grilled Yukon Potato Wedges

SERVES 4 TO 6 / **PREP TIME:** 30 to 45 minutes / **COOK TIME:** 1 to 1½ hours
SUGGESTED WOOD: Apple wood chunk

These bacon-wrapped potato wedges are a hearty and filling side dish for any main entrée. Smoky and rich bacon wrapped around a soft, creamy potato wedge is what side-dish dreams are made of. Dip them in the Smoked Garlic Aioli and you'll be in potato bliss!

3 to 4 large Yukon Gold potatoes
Avocado oil spray
1 tablespoon SPJG Rub (page 194)
1 (12-ounce) package bacon
2 tablespoons chopped fresh chives
Smoked Garlic Aioli (page 203), for serving

1. Set up your grill for indirect cooking (see page 4). Fill a charcoal chimney with lump charcoal and light it with a fire starter cube. When the coals have turned gray, dump them into the grill on the side opposite the disposable aluminum pan, replace the cooking grate, close the lid, and open the top and bottom vents until the grill temperature registers about 300°F. Continue to monitor the grill, adjusting the vents as needed, until it reaches a cooking temperature of 325°F to 350°F.

2. With a fork, poke a few holes on all sides of the potatoes, then spray each with avocado oil and sprinkle with the rub. Tightly wrap each potato in aluminum foil and set aside.

3. When the grill is ready, open the lid, place the potatoes on the indirect side, close the lid, and cook for 30 minutes. After 30 minutes, remove the potatoes to a cutting board and let rest for 10 to 15 minutes. About 15 minutes before you plan to finish cooking the potatoes, place an applewood chunk on the coals.

4. After the potatoes have rested, remove the foil and cut each potato into 6 wedges. The potatoes may be hot and still firm. Wrap a slice of bacon around each potato wedge and secure it with a toothpick. Repeat until all the wedges are wrapped, then season with the rub.

5. Place the wedges on the indirect side of the grill over the drip pan, close the lid, and cook for 15 minutes. Open the lid and rotate the wedges 180 degrees, close the lid, and cook for another 15 minutes, or until the bacon is crispy.

6. Remove the potato wedges from the grill and place them on a serving tray. Top with chopped chives and serve with the aioli.

PRO TIP: You want the potatoes to be slightly firm when you slice them into wedges so they do not crumble apart when they're wrapped with bacon. When testing for tenderness, use the end of an instant-read thermometer; it should probe with some resistance.

Hawaiian Mac Salad

SERVES 4 TO 6 / **PREP TIME:** 5 to 10 minutes / **COOK TIME:** 12 to 15 minutes, plus resting time

When I was stationed on Oahu during my service in the US Navy, this macaroni salad was a staple on lunch plates across the island. The rich, creamy texture pairs perfectly with sweet, sticky, charred meats. Honey Teriyaki Kalbi Beef Short Ribs (page 42), Sticky Honey Teriyaki Baby Back Ribs (page 80), Huli-Huli Style Chicken (page 114), Chicken Yakitori Skewers (page 122), and Hawaiian Pork Kabobs with Sweet Maui Onion and Pineapple (page 90) are all great main dishes for this side. Add a scoop of white rice for a proper Hawaiian lunch plate.

1 (16-ounce) box elbow macaroni
½ sweet Maui onion
2 cups mayonnaise
1 tablespoon SPGJ Rub (page 194)

1. Prepare the macaroni according to package instructions, making sure not to overcook it. Drain and set aside to cool.

2. Grate the onion using a cheese grater (it will be pretty liquidy) into a large bowl. Add the mayonnaise and the rub and stir to combine thoroughly. When the drained noodles have cooled a bit, add them to the mayonnaise and toss to evenly coat. Cover with plastic wrap and refrigerate for 1 to 2 hours to bring out the flavors.

3. After the macaroni has chilled, remove from the refrigerator and serve.

> **PRO TIP:** Grate the onion in the same bowl you will place the macaroni in once it has cooled to catch all the onion juices.

Agave-Glazed Carrots

SERVES 4 TO 6 / PREP TIME: 5 to 10 minutes / **COOK TIME:** 20 to 25 minutes

I like to use multicolored or rainbow carrots for this recipe, which add a great color contrast. These carrots are a perfect side for prime rib, rack of pork, and other large family-style meals.

1 or 2 bunches
   rainbow carrots

4 tablespoons (½ stick)
   salted butter

2 tablespoons
   agave nectar

2 tablespoons light
   brown sugar

½ teaspoon grated
   fresh ginger

Salt

Freshly ground
   black pepper

2 tablespoons
   sliced almonds

1. Cut the top inch off of each carrot and discard.

2. In a saucepan over medium-high heat, melt the butter. When the butter is melted, add the carrots and cook for 10 minutes, tossing frequently. Reduce the heat to medium and add the agave, brown sugar, and ginger. Toss to coat the carrots and cook for another 10 minutes, making sure not to boil or burn the carrots. If the mixture starts to boil, reduce the heat to medium-low. Cook until the carrots are fork-tender. Add salt and pepper to taste.

3. Place the carrots on a serving tray. Spoon any leftover agave glaze over the carrots and top with sliced almonds. Serve and enjoy!

GRILLED ROMAINE HEARTS WITH CANDIED BACON, CAESAR DRESSING, AND PARMESAN

SERVES 4 TO 6 / **PREP TIME:** 30 to 45 minutes / **COOK TIME:** 1 to 2 minutes

This grilled salad recipe is from my good friend Johan Magnusson from Big Swede BBQ. We have taught multiple barbecue classes together, and I always love it when he makes this salad in class. The Caesar dressing pairs perfectly with the chargrilled lettuce. Add the candied bacon and Parmesan cheese and this salad is next level.

For the Caesar dressing

6 anchovy fillets packed in oil, drained and finely chopped

1 garlic clove, minced

Salt

2 large egg yolks

2 tablespoons lemon juice, plus more to taste

¾ teaspoon Dijon mustard

1 teaspoon hot sauce

1 teaspoon Worcestershire sauce

2 tablespoons vegetable oil

½ cup extra-virgin olive oil

3 tablespoons finely grated Parmesan cheese

Pinch freshly ground black pepper

1. **TO MAKE THE CAESAR DRESSING:** In a small bowl, use the back of a spoon or fork to mash the anchovies, garlic, and a pinch of salt into a paste. Work them into each other for a minute or two to incorporate. Scrape the anchovy-garlic paste into a medium bowl. Whisk in the egg yolks, lemon juice, and Dijon mustard. Add the hot sauce and Worcestershire sauce and whisk for 1 minute. Gradually whisk in the vegetable oil, then the olive oil, and continue to whisk until the dressing is thick and glossy. Add the Parmesan cheese and season with a pinch of pepper and more salt and lemon juice, if desired. Whisk again to combine, then cover and refrigerate until ready to serve.

2. **TO MAKE THE SALAD:** Set up your grill for direct cooking (see page 3). Fill a charcoal chimney with charcoal and light it with a fire starter cube. When the coals have turned gray, dump them into the grill grate or basket in an even layer. Replace the cooking grate, add GrillGrates to the grill, flat-side up, close the lid, then open the top and bottom vents. You are looking for the grill temperature to be at least 450°F (this will take 20 to 30 minutes).

For the salad

3 or 4 romaine hearts,
  rinsed, dried,
  and halved

Avocado oil spray

Salt

Freshly ground
  black pepper

4 to 6 slices Spicy
  Candied Bacon
  (page 27), crumbled

Shaved Parmesan
  cheese, for serving

3. Spray the cut side of each romaine heart with avocado oil, season with salt and pepper, and set aside.

4. When the grill is hot, place the romaine hearts cut-side down evenly across the grill. Cook for 1 to 2 minutes, until you see visible grill marks, making sure not to burn the lettuce.

5. When the hearts have a nice char, remove them from the grill to a serving platter. Let rest for 5 minutes.

6. To serve, top the hearts with Caesar dressing, crumbled candied bacon, and shaved Parmesan.

Seasoned Turnip Wedges with Goat Cheese and Balsamic

SERVES 4 TO 6 / PREP TIME: 30 to 45 minutes / **COOK TIME:** 25 to 35 minutes
SUGGESTED WOOD: Pecan wood chunk

Turnips are very similar to carrots in terms of texture, and they have an earthy, potato-like taste. When grilled, they have a sweet flavor, much like carrots, that comes out. I like using the Vortex barbecue ring when cooking these, because the heat radiates around the grill and creates a nice crust on the turnip wedges.

3 or 4 turnips, peeled

2 tablespoons extra-virgin olive oil, divided

1 tablespoon Poultry and Seafood Rub (page 196), divided

Avocado oil spray

¼ cup balsamic glaze

½ cup crumbled goat cheese

3 or 4 fresh basil leaves, rolled and sliced (chiffonade)

1. Cut each turnip in half, then cut each half into thirds. Place the turnip wedges in a large bowl and drizzle with 1 tablespoon of olive oil and the rub. Toss the wedges to coat evenly. Set aside.

2. Set up your grill for indirect cooking (see page 4). Fill a charcoal chimney with lump charcoal and light it with a fire starter cube. When the coals have turned gray, dump them into the grill on the side opposite the disposable aluminum pan, replace the cooking grate, close the lid, and open the top and bottom vents until the grill temperature registers about 350°F. Continue to monitor the grill, adjusting the vents as needed, until it reaches a cooking temperature of 375°F to 400°F. If you're using a Vortex unit, set it up as recommended, with the unit in the middle of the grill. About 15 minutes before you plan to cook, place a small pecan wood chunk on the hot coals, then close the lid.

3. When the grill is up to temperature and the smoke is clean, open the lid and place the turnip wedges on the indirect side of the grill over the drip pan or around

the Vortex. Close the lid and cook for 15 minutes. Open the lid, spray the wedges with avocado oil, and rotate or flip them for even cooking. Replace the lid and cook for another 10 to 15 minutes. Open the lid and check the turnips for doneness. You want them to be tender but not mushy in the center, with a nice golden, crisp exterior.

4. When the wedges are done, remove them from the grill to a serving plate and let rest for 5 minutes.

5. After resting, drizzle the wedges with the remaining 1 tablespoon of olive oil and the balsamic glaze, and sprinkle crumbled goat cheese and basil on top. Serve and enjoy!

PRO TIP: I like to test the turnips for doneness by eating one. When the wedges start to get a nice crisp exterior, I pull one off the grill, rest it for a minute, and bite into it to check the texture. I like mine with a little bite but still tender.

Smoked Buffalo Cauliflower

SERVES 4 TO 6 / **PREP TIME:** 20 to 25 minutes / **COOK TIME:** 1 to 1½ hours
SUGGESTED WOOD: Pecan wood chunks

Cooking the whole cauliflower head on the grill is my favorite way to eat it. I love how the cauliflower accepts the smoke flavor, which gives it a meaty taste.

1 head cauliflower

4 tablespoons (½ stick) salted butter

1 cup hot sauce, preferably Frank's RedHot

2 tablespoons honey

1 tablespoon Dijon mustard

Classic White BBQ Sauce (page 200), for serving

¼ cup chopped fresh parsley

1. Trim the leaves around the bottom and the stem of the cauliflower so it stands upright. Wash and pat it dry with paper towels.

2. In a saucepan over medium-high heat, melt the butter, then add the hot sauce, honey, and Dijon mustard. Reduce the heat to medium and stir to combine. When the ingredients are heated through and incorporated, remove the pan from the heat and set aside.

3. Set up your grill for indirect cooking (see page 4). Fill a charcoal chimney with lump charcoal and light it with a fire starter cube. When the coals have turned gray, dump them into the grill on the side opposite the disposable aluminum pan, replace the cooking grate, close the lid, and open the top and bottom vents until the grill temperature registers about 300°F. Continue to monitor the grill, adjusting the vents as needed, until it reaches a cooking temperature of 325°F to 350°F. About 15 minutes before you plan to cook, place a small pecan wood chunk on the hot coals, then close the lid.

4. Make sure the cauliflower is dry, then starting at the top, brush half the butter–hot sauce mixture all over the cauliflower.

5. When the grill is ready, open the lid and place the cauliflower stem-side down on the indirect side of the grill. Close the lid and cook for 30 minutes. Open the lid and rotate the cauliflower 180 degrees, brush again with the butter–hot sauce mixture, close the lid, and cook for another 30 minutes. Open the lid, rotate the cauliflower, brush with the remaining butter–hot sauce, and test for doneness using the end of an instant-read thermometer. You are looking for the cauliflower to probe smoothly with very little to no resistance. If it is tough and not probing smoothly, close the lid and cook for another 15 minutes, then test again.

6. When the cauliflower is ready, remove it from the grill to a cutting board and let rest for 5 to 10 minutes.

7. To serve, slice the cauliflower into 1-inch-thick "steaks." Lay them on a serving plate, drizzle with white sauce, and top with chopped parsley.

LOADED GRILLED POTATO BOATS

SERVES 4 TO 6 / PREP TIME: 20 to 25 minutes / **COOK TIME:** 1 to 1½ hours

I love potatoes, and this is one of my favorite ways to eat them. Loaded with cream cheese and sharp cheddar cheese, these creamy, cheesy potato boats are a perfect side dish or appetizer.

2 or 3 large russet
  potatoes
Avocado oil spray
1 tablespoon SPGJ Rub
  (page 194)
4 ounces cream cheese
½ cup shredded sharp
  cheddar cheese
¼ cup heavy cream
¼ cup sour cream
2 tablespoons
  salted butter
4 to 6 slices Spicy
  Candied Bacon
  (page 27), crumbled
¼ cup chopped
  fresh chives

1. With a fork, poke a few holes about 1 inch deep in the center of the potatoes and spray them with avocado oil. Season with the rub and wrap each potato in aluminum foil.

2. Set up your grill for indirect cooking (see page 4). Fill a charcoal chimney with lump charcoal and light it with a fire starter cube. When the coals have turned gray, dump them into the grill on the side opposite the disposable aluminum pan, replace the cooking grate, close the lid, and open the top and bottom vents until the grill temperature registers about 300°F. Continue to monitor the grill, adjusting the vents as needed, until it reaches a cooking temperature of 325°F to 350°F.

3. When the grill is ready, place the potatoes on the indirect side of the grill. Close the lid and cook for 30 to 45 minutes. Open the lid and test the tenderness of the potato with the end of an instant-read thermometer. You are looking for the thermometer to slide into the potato with very little to no resistance. If needed, continue to cook the potatoes for 15 minutes, then test again. When the potatoes are tender, remove them from the grill and let rest for 10 minutes.

4. While the potatoes are resting, combine the cream cheese, shredded cheddar, heavy cream, sour cream, butter, and 2 teaspoons of the rub in a large bowl. After the potatoes have rested, remove the foil and slice them in half to create two "boats." With a spoon, carefully remove the potato flesh from the skin, leaving ¼ inch of potato inside the skin, and add the scooped-out potato to the bowl with the cream cheese mixture. Repeat until all the potatoes are scooped. With a large spoon or hand mixer, combine the potatoes and cream cheese mixture thoroughly.

5. Set the potato boats on a plate and evenly divide the potato filling among the boats. Place them on the indirect side of the grill over the drip tray. Close the lid and cook for 20 to 25 minutes to heat through. Remove them from the grill and top with crumbled candied bacon and chopped chives. Serve and dig in!

Mesquite Grilled Salsa

SERVES 4 TO 6 / **PREP TIME:** 10 to 15 minutes / **COOK TIME:** 10 to 15 minutes
SUGGESTED WOOD: Mesquite lump charcoal

This salsa can be used in many different ways and in many recipes. Use it as an appetizer with chips and sliced veggies or a topping for tacos, enchiladas, and tostadas, or add it to omelets or any other protein for a fresh Southwestern kick.

5 or 6 Roma tomatoes
1 medium white onion
1 head garlic
1 jalapeño, stemmed
1 serrano
  pepper, stemmed
1 tablespoon extra-virgin
  olive oil
2 teaspoons
  Southwestern
  Seasoning
  (page 197), divided
1 bunch cilantro,
  chopped, divided
½ cup chicken stock
Juice of 1 lime
Salt
Freshly ground
  black pepper

1. Halve the Roma tomatoes lengthwise, quarter the onion, and cut the top off of the head of garlic. Place the tomatoes, onion, garlic, jalapeño, and serrano pepper in a mixing bowl and toss with the olive oil and 1 teaspoon seasoning mix. Set the vegetables aside while you prepare the grill.

2. Set up your grill for direct cooking (see page 3). Fill a charcoal chimney with mesquite lump charcoal and light it with a fire starter cube. When the coals have turned gray, dump them into the grill grate or basket in an even layer. Replace the cooking grate, add GrillGrates to the grill flat-side up, close the lid, and open the top and bottom vents. You are looking for the grill temperature to be at least 450°F (this will take 20 to 30 minutes).

3. When the grill is ready, place the tomatoes, onions, garlic, jalapeño, and serrano pepper evenly around the grill. Cook for 3 to 5 minutes, then rotate or flip the vegetables to get a char on each side. Cook for another 3 to 5 minutes. If some of the vegetables are getting too charred, move them to a large glass bowl and cover

with plastic wrap. When all the vegetables are charred, place them in the large bowl and cover with plastic wrap to rest for 15 to 20 minutes.

4. Take out the head of garlic and remove the cloves, discarding the peel. In the bowl of a food processor or blender, combine the garlic cloves, tomatoes, onion, peppers, ½ cup of cilantro, the chicken stock, any leftover juices from the resting bowl, and the remaining 1 teaspoon of the seasoning mix. Pulse or blend until you have a smooth yet chunky consistency. Add the lime juice and salt and black pepper to taste. Pour the salsa back into the holding bowl, cover with plastic wrap, and place in the refrigerator. Serve chilled.

LUCKY HOPPIN' JOHN WITH SMOKED PORK SHANK

SERVES 4 TO 6 / **PREP TIME:** 10 to 15 minutes / **COOK TIME:** 6 hours

This recipe is a New Year's Day tradition in our house. I make it with canned black-eyed peas, but you can also use dried peas. It is an easy recipe, as you dump everything into a slow cooker and let time and heat do all the work.

4 (16-ounce) cans black-eyed peas, drained and rinsed

1 medium white onion, diced

1 jalapeño, diced

2 smoked pork shanks

2 tablespoons SPGJ Rub (page 194)

2 cups chicken stock, plus more as needed

1. Set up your slow cooker for a low and slow cook. Add the black-eyed peas, onion, jalapeño, pork shanks, and seasoning and stir. Pour in enough chicken stock to just cover all ingredients. Place the lid on and cook for 6 hours.

2. When the pork shank shreds off the bone easily, it is done.

3. Discard bones and serve over a bowl of white rice for luck all year long.

BAKED BEANS WITH BACON

SERVES 4 TO 6 / **PREP TIME:** 15 to 20 minutes / **COOK TIME:** 2 to 2½ hours

I like using my cast-iron pan for this recipe and letting the beans soak up the grill flavor. Make sure to use thick-cut bacon, as the fat will render slowly and flavor the beans throughout the cook time. For an awesome presentation, place warmed leftover brisket burnt ends or pulled pork in the middle of the cast-iron pan before serving.

4 (16-ounce) cans baked beans
1 medium onion, diced
2 or 3 serrano peppers
Avocado oil spray
1 (12-ounce) package thick-cut bacon
½ cup packed light brown sugar
1 to 2 tablespoons Sweet and Savory Rub (page 195)

PRO TIP: Try this recipe with leftover brisket burnt ends or chunks instead of bacon for another level of flavor. The fatty, rich brisket will add a deep smoky flavor to the beans.

1. Set up your grill for indirect cooking (see page 4). Fill a charcoal chimney with lump charcoal and light it with a fire starter cube. When the coals have turned gray, dump them into the grill on the side opposite the disposable aluminum pan, replace the cooking grate, close the lid, and open the top and bottom vents until the grill temperature registers about 300°F. Continue to monitor the grill, adjusting the vents as needed, until it reaches a cooking temperature of 325°F to 350°F.

2. Combine the baked beans, diced onion, and whole serrano peppers in a disposable aluminum half pan or cast-iron skillet sprayed with avocado oil. Stir to combine thoroughly. Lay the thick-cut bacon strips across the pan or skillet in parallel lines, leaving an inch between strips. Sprinkle the brown sugar over the bacon strips, then top with the rub.

3. When the grill is ready, open the lid and place the pan on the indirect side of the grill. Close the lid and cook for 30 minutes. Open the lid, rotate the pan 180 degrees, close the lid, and cook for another 30 minutes. After 1 hour of cooking, open the lid and check to make sure the bacon is rendering and caramelizing. The beans should be bubbling and hot. When the beans are done and the bacon is caramelized, remove the pan from the grill and set aside to rest for 5 to 10 minutes, then serve and enjoy!

Roasted Vegetable Basket

MAKES 4 TO 6 / **PREP TIME:** 10 to 15 minutes / **COOK TIME:** 30 minutes

We make this veggie basket at least three or four nights a week at home. It goes with everything, and you can season it for any occasion or main dish pairing. I use a metal grilling basket easily found at hardware stores or online for this recipe. It is a handy barbecue tool to have, as it keeps small items like vegetables, shrimp, and bacon slices from falling into the grill.

1 large red onion

1 large zucchini

1 large yellow squash

1 large red bell pepper

1 bunch asparagus

1 jalapeño

1 (8-ounce) package whole portobello mushrooms

8 to 12 garlic cloves, peeled

2 tablespoons extra-virgin olive oil

2 tablespoons SPGJ Rub (page 194), plus more as needed

1. Set up your grill for indirect cooking (see page 4). Fill a charcoal chimney with lump charcoal and light it with a fire starter cube. When the coals have turned gray, dump them into the grill on the side opposite the disposable aluminum pan, replace the cooking grate, close the lid, and open the top and bottom vents until the grill temperature registers about 300°F. Continue to monitor the grill, adjusting the vents as needed, until it reaches a cooking temperature of 325°F to 350°F. Place the cooking basket on the indirect side of the grill and close the lid.

2. While the grill is getting up to temperature, lay the vegetables out on a cutting board. Slice the onion, zucchini, squash, and bell pepper into uniform medium pieces. Trim the bottoms off the asparagus and slice the spears in half. Slice the jalapeño into uniform disks. Trim and discard the stems from the mushrooms and keep the caps whole. Place all the veggies and whole garlic cloves in a large bowl. Add the olive oil and the rub and stir to combine thoroughly.

3. When the grill is ready, open the lid and pour the vegetables from the mixing bowl into the grill basket. With tongs, move them around so they are evenly distributed in the basket. Close the lid and cook for 15 minutes. Open the lid, rotate the basket 180 degrees, and give the veggies a toss with the tongs. Close the lid and cook for another 10 minutes. Open the lid, give the veggies another toss, then with your tongs, move the basket to the direct-heat side. Cook for 1 to 2 minutes, toss the vegetables, and cook for another 1 to 2 minutes, until the vegetables have caramelized and are charred but not burnt.

4. When the vegetables are done, remove the basket from the grill and let rest for 5 minutes. Taste and add more of the rub if needed.

5. Serve alongside your favorite main dish or just grab a fork and have at it!

PRO TIP: Try these vegetables topped with olive oil, balsamic glaze, feta cheese, and chopped fresh basil.

Brown Sugar and Pecan Sweet Potatoes

SERVES 4 TO 6 / **PREP TIME:** 15 to 20 minutes / **COOK TIME:** 1 to 1½ hours
SUGGESTED WOOD: Pecan wood chunk

I love cooking this recipe around the holidays to serve alongside ham, turkey, or prime rib. The sweet potatoes pair well with brown sugar and butter, and the pecans add a nice texture and crunch.

6 medium sweet
potatoes, washed
and dried
Avocado oil spray
Salt
8 tablespoons (1 stick)
salted butter, cut into
pat-size pieces
1 cup packed light
brown sugar
1 cup chopped pecans
½ teaspoon ground
cinnamon

1. Set up your grill for indirect cooking (see page 4). Fill a charcoal chimney with lump charcoal and light it with a fire starter cube. When the coals have turned gray, dump them into the grill on the side opposite the disposable aluminum pan, replace the cooking grate, close the lid, and open the top and bottom vents until the grill temperature registers about 300°F. Continue to monitor the grill, adjusting the vents as needed, until it reaches a cooking temperature of 325°F to 350°F. About 15 minutes before you plan to grill, place 1 or 2 small pecan wood chunks directly on the hot coals, then close the lid.

2. While the grill is getting up to temperature, cut the sweet potatoes into 1½-inch chunks. Spray a disposable aluminum half pan with avocado oil. Place the sweet potatoes in the pan, sprinkle with salt, spray the potatoes with avocado oil, and toss, then cover the pan with aluminum foil and place it on the indirect side of the grill. Close the lid and cook for 25 minutes. Open the lid, rotate the pan 180 degrees, close the lid, and cook for another 20 to 25 minutes, then take the pan off the grill. Remove the aluminum foil and give the potatoes a stir. Place the pats of butter evenly on top of the potatoes and sprinkle the brown sugar, chopped pecans, and cinnamon all over the potatoes. Sprinkle

with salt and place the pan, uncovered, back on the indirect side of the grill for 20 to 30 minutes with the lid closed. Test the potatoes for doneness by tasting one or inserting an instant-read thermometer into a piece. The potato should probe fairly easily with no resistance and the brown sugar and butter should be melted through. Give the potatoes a stir and continue to cook until tender.

3. When the potatoes are done, remove them from the grill, give them a stir, and let rest for 5 to 10 minutes.

4. Place the sweet potatoes on a serving dish and pour the melted butter and brown sugar on top. Serve and enjoy!

Grilled Beet Chopped Caprese Salad

SERVES 4 TO 6 / **PREP TIME:** 10 to 15 minutes / **COOK TIME:** 20 to 25 minutes

Adding grilled beets to this caprese salad is a must. The flavor the beets pick up from the grill adds to their natural sweetness, and the heat helps caramelize the outside. I like to serve this fresh, crisp salad with rich fatty meats like brisket and pulled pork.

4 or 5 medium beets, peeled

Avocado oil spray

1 tablespoon salt, plus more to taste

1 tablespoon sugar

1 (8-ounce) ball fresh mozzarella cheese

4 or 5 Roma tomatoes, cored and seeded

6 to 8 fresh basil leaves, cut into chiffonade or chopped

1 tablespoon extra-virgin olive oil

1 to 2 tablespoons balsamic glaze

1. Set up your grill for direct cooking (see page 3). Fill a charcoal chimney with charcoal and light it with a fire starter cube. When the coals have turned gray, dump them into the grill grate or basket in an even layer, replace the cooking grate, close the lid, and open the top and bottom vents. You are looking for the grill temperature to be at least 450°F (this takes 20 to 30 minutes).

2. Slice the beets into ½-inch-thick disks. Spray both sides with avocado oil, then sprinkle lightly with the salt and sugar.

3. When the grill is ready, open the lid and place the beet slices evenly around the grill. Close the lid and cook for 10 to 12 minutes. Open the lid, spray them with avocado oil, and flip. Close the lid and cook for another 10 to 12 minutes. You are looking for the beets to be caramelized but not burnt.

4. When done, remove the beets to a plate. Cover with aluminum foil and let rest for 5 minutes. While they are resting, cut the mozzarella into ½-inch cubes and dice the tomatoes into ½-inch cubes. Place the mozzarella and tomatoes in a large bowl, add the basil leaves, drizzle with the olive oil, and stir to combine. Place the beets on a cutting board and slice them into ½-inch cubes, add them the mixing bowl, and toss to combine. Add salt to taste. Drizzle the balsamic glaze over the beets and serve.

Bacon-Wrapped Asparagus

SERVES 4 TO 6 / **PREP TIME:** 20 to 30 minutes / **COOK TIME:** 25 to 30 minutes
SUGGESTED WOOD: Pecan wood chunk

I've featured this recipe in several barbecue classes that I have taught across the country. It is easy to make yet very flavorful. The fatty, crispy bacon and the citrus mayo are great accompaniments to the asparagus.

1 bunch asparagus
1 (12-ounce) package
   thin-sliced bacon
1 tablespoon SPGJ Rub
   (page 194)
¾ cup mayonnaise
Juice of 1 lemon
1 tablespoon extra-virgin
   olive oil
2 teaspoons
   lemon-pepper
   seasoning

> **PRO TIP:** Wrap the asparagus with thin-sliced bacon to make sure it renders while the asparagus is cooked perfectly inside.

1. Lay the asparagus on a cutting board and cut off the bottom ends. Stack them in groups of three or four. Wrap a piece of bacon around the middle of each asparagus stack. Repeat until all the asparagus is wrapped. Season them with the rub and set aside.

2. In a bowl, combine the mayonnaise, lemon juice, olive oil, and lemon-pepper and stir to blend thoroughly. Cover and refrigerate until ready to serve.

3. Set up your grill for indirect cooking (see page 4). Fill a charcoal chimney with lump charcoal and light it with a fire starter cube. When the coals have turned gray, dump them into the grill on the side opposite the disposable aluminum pan, replace the cooking grate, close the lid, and open the top and bottom vents until the grill temperature registers about 300°F. Continue to monitor the grill, adjusting the vents as needed, until it reaches a 325°F to 350°F. About 15 minutes before you plan to cook, place a medium pecan wood chunk directly on the hot coals, then close the lid.

4. When the grill is up to temperature, place the asparagus wraps on the indirect side, close the lid, and cook for 15 minutes. Open the lid, rotate and flip the asparagus wraps, then close the lid and cook for 10 to 15 minutes more, until the bacon is cooked.

5. Remove the asparagus wraps from the grill to a platter. Serve with the citrus mayo on the side.

CHEESY SHREDDED POTATO CASSEROLE

SERVES 4 TO 6 / **PREP TIME:** 10 to 15 minutes / **COOK TIME:** 40 to 45 minutes

These potatoes are so cheesy and creamy. You can cook them in your oven or on the grill in a disposable aluminum pan. I like using one diced jalapeño in mine, but if you prefer less heat use half a jalapeño, or if you like more, use a couple in the dish.

Avocado oil spray

1 (20-ounce) bag shredded potatoes

1 (16-ounce) can cream of chicken soup

1 cup shredded sharp cheddar cheese

2 tablespoons salted butter, melted

¼ cup diced white onion

1 jalapeño, diced

2 tablespoons SPGJ Rub (page 194)

¼ cup diced scallions

1. Spray a 9-by-9-inch glass baking dish with avocado oil and set aside. Preheat your oven or grill to 350°F. If grilling, use an indirect setup (see page 4).

2. In a large bowl, combine the shredded potatoes, cream of chicken soup, cheddar cheese, melted butter, onion, jalapeño, and the rub. Stir to combine thoroughly.

3. Pour the mixture into the prepared baking dish and smooth the top. Cover with aluminum foil and cook for 25 to 30 minutes. Remove the foil and cook for another 15 minutes, or until it is bubbling and golden brown on top.

4. Let the potatoes rest uncovered for 5 to 10 minutes.

5. Top with chopped scallions and serve.

Chopped Mediterranean Salad with Homemade Tzatziki Sauce

SERVES 4 TO 6 / **PREP TIME:** 25 to 30 minutes

This tzatziki sauce is amazing on many things, not just this salad. I use it on my Ultimate Lamb Burger (page 58) and with the gyro skewers recipe (page 60). The creamy, tangy, zippy sauce is a perfect match for the fresh salad.

For the tzatziki sauce

1 cucumber, peeled and shredded

2 teaspoons salt, divided

3 garlic cloves, finely grated

2 cups Greek yogurt

Juice of 1 lemon

2 or 3 mint leaves, chopped

2 teaspoons freshly ground black pepper

For the salad

1 head iceberg lettuce, chopped

2 or 3 Roma tomatoes, diced

1 cucumber, diced

1 small white onion, diced

5 or 6 kalamata olives, pitted and sliced

Crumbled feta cheese

1. **TO MAKE THE TZATZIKI SAUCE:** Place the shredded cucumber in a bowl and sprinkle 1 teaspoon of salt on top. Set aside for 10 minutes to allow the salt to draw out excess moisture from the cucumber. Place the cucumber in a clean piece of cheesecloth or kitchen towel. Over your sink, twist the cloth to squeeze as much liquid as you can from the cucumber. You want it as dry as possible to avoid a runny sauce.

2. Place the cucumber in a bowl and add the grated garlic, Greek yogurt, lemon juice, mint, the remaining 1 teaspoon of salt, and the pepper. Mix thoroughly to combine. Cover and refrigerate until you're ready to serve.

3. **TO MAKE THE SALAD:** Place the lettuce, tomatoes, cucumber, onion, and olives in a large bowl and toss to mix. Sprinkle the crumbled feta cheese over the salad, drizzle with tzatziki sauce, and serve.

RUBS, BRINES, MARINADES, AND SAUCES

◀ Championship Pork
Spareribs (page 72)

SPGJ Rub

MAKES APPROXIMATELY 1¼ CUPS / **PREP TIME:** 5 minutes

This all-purpose rub pairs best with proteins like beef and lamb but also works well with potatoes and other vegetables.

½ cup kosher salt

½ cup coarsely ground
   black pepper

¼ cup garlic powder

2 tablespoons jalapeño
   pepper flakes

1 tablespoon red
   pepper flakes

Combine all the ingredients in a bowl and mix thoroughly. Transfer to a shaker bottle with a sealable lid. Store in a cool, dry place for up to one month.

> **USE WITH:** This is a true all-purpose seasoning and can be used for almost everything: beef, lamb, venison, pork, poultry, seafood, and vegetables.

Sweet and Savory Rub

MAKES APPROXIMATELY 1½ CUPS / PREP TIME: 5 minutes

I like to use this sweet and savory seasoning on all things pork. Bacon, ribs, tenderloin, and pretty much every cut works well with this rub.

½ cup turbinado sugar

¼ cup kosher salt

¼ cup packed light brown sugar

3 tablespoons smoked paprika

1 tablespoon freshly ground black pepper

1 tablespoon onion powder

1 tablespoon garlic powder

1 tablespoon red pepper flakes

Combine all the ingredients in a bowl and mix thoroughly. Transfer to a shaker bottle with a sealable lid. Store in a cool, dry place for up to one month.

USE WITH: This seasoning pairs perfectly with pork.

POULTRY AND SEAFOOD RUB

MAKES APPROXIMATELY 1½ CUPS / **PREP TIME:** 5 minutes

If you prefer less heat, simply use less chili powder or cayenne pepper.

½ cup kosher salt

¼ cup garlic powder

¼ cup granulated onion

1 tablespoon sugar

1 tablespoon Italian
  seasoning

1 tablespoon chili powder

1 tablespoon
  lemon-pepper
  seasoning

1 tablespoon
  smoked paprika

1 teaspoon
  cayenne pepper

1 teaspoon
  mustard powder

1 teaspoon celery seed

Combine all the ingredients in a bowl and mix thoroughly. Transfer to a shaker bottle with a sealable lid. Store in a cool, dry place for up to one month.

USE WITH: This herby, salty seasoning with a back-end kick pairs well with all types of poultry and seafood.

SOUTHWESTERN SEASONING

MAKES APPROXIMATELY 1½ CUPS / PREP TIME: 5 minutes

This seasoning is perfect for carne asada meats like flank and skirt steaks.

½ cup kosher salt

¼ cup smoked paprika

¼ cup garlic powder

2 tablespoons
  onion powder

1 tablespoon
  lemon-pepper
  seasoning

1 tablespoon chili powder

1 tablespoon
  ground cumin

1 tablespoon jalapeño
  pepper flakes

1 teaspoon
  cayenne pepper

1 teaspoon sugar

Combine all the ingredients in a bowl and mix thoroughly. Transfer to a shaker bottle with a sealable lid. Store in a cool, dry place for up to one month.

USE WITH: Try this with all types of proteins, including skirt and flank steaks, poultry, and seafood. I have also used this in ground meat for tacos, in guacamole, on vegetables, and on grilled pineapple.

STICKY HONEY TERIYAKI SAUCE

MAKES APPROXIMATELY 1½ CUPS / PREP TIME: 10 minutes / **COOK TIME:** 1 minute

This is one of my favorite sauces. We use it for multiple recipes and my kids love the sweet honey flavor. I make a double batch for most recipes and save some to use in a different dish later in the week or as a dipping sauce.

½ cup soy sauce

¼ cup pineapple juice

¼ cup honey

¼ cup packed light brown sugar

2 or 3 garlic cloves, minced

1 teaspoon minced fresh ginger

1 teaspoon toasted sesame oil

½ teaspoon sriracha

2 tablespoons cornstarch

¼ cup water

Pinch salt (optional)

1. In a saucepan over medium heat, combine the soy sauce, pineapple juice, honey, brown sugar, garlic, ginger, sesame oil, and sriracha. Cook until heated through, about 1 minute.

2. In a small mixing bowl combine the cornstarch and water, whisking well to dissolve the cornstarch, then add it to the saucepan. Heat the sauce through over medium-low heat, making sure not to burn it or let it boil. Taste and add a pinch of salt, if necessary.

USE WITH: Honey Teriyaki Kalbi Beef Short Ribs (page 42), Sticky Honey Teriyaki Baby Back Ribs (page 80), Hawaiian Pork Kabobs with Sweet Maui Onion and Pineapple (page 90), Huli-Huli Style Chicken (page 114), Chicken Yakitori Skewers (page 122)

SOUTHWEST SWEET HEAT BBQ SAUCE

MAKES APPROXIMATELY 2½ CUPS / PREP TIME: 10 minutes
COOK TIME: About 5 minutes

This sauce is my version of a Kansas City–style barbecue sauce with a little of the Southwest mixed in. It is a traditional tomato-based, brown sugar and molasses sauce kicked up with chipotles in adobo and cayenne pepper. You can adjust the heat level and add as much or little spice as you want.

1 cup ketchup

½ cup packed light
  brown sugar

¼ cup water

¼ cup apple cider vinegar

¼ cup molasses

¼ cup peach syrup from a
  can of peaches (reserve
  the peaches to use in a
  different recipe)

2 tablespoons
  yellow mustard

2 tablespoons honey

1 chipotle chile in adobo
  sauce, finely diced

1½ teaspoons
  onion powder

1½ teaspoons
  garlic powder

1 teaspoon salt

1 teaspoon freshly ground
  black pepper

1 teaspoon
  cayenne pepper

In a saucepan over medium heat, combine all the ingredients and heat through, about 5 minutes, making sure not to burn the sauce. If it is too thick, use water or apple juice to thin it to the desired consistency.

USE WITH: Pork Belly Pimento Cheese Bites (page 18), Championship Pork Spareribs (page 72), Pork Tenderloin Pinwheels à la Richard Fergola (page 78), Thick-Cut Pork Steak (page 96), Bacon-Wrapped Mozzarella-Stuffed Boneless Chicken Thighs (page 118), and Spatchcocked BBQ Chicken (page 120)

CLASSIC WHITE BBQ SAUCE

MAKES APPROXIMATELY 1½ CUPS / PREP TIME: 5 minutes

This sauce takes me back to my time living in Columbus, Georgia. We loved to visit Big Bob Gibson Bar-B-Q in Alabama, where the chicken with white sauce was my favorite menu item. This is my version of this classic Southern sauce.

1 cup mayonnaise

¼ cup apple cider vinegar

Juice of 1 lemon

1 tablespoon
  Dijon mustard

1 tablespoon prepared
  horseradish

1 teaspoon freshly ground
  black pepper

½ teaspoon ancho
  chile powder

Pinch salt

Combine all the ingredients in a large bowl and mix thoroughly. Store in the refrigerator until needed, then warm in a microwave or on the stovetop before use.

USE WITH: Chicken Wings with White BBQ Sauce (page 23), Salt and Pepper Duck Wings (page 130), Mesquite Grilled Whole Rainbow Trout (page 159)

CARNE AND POLLO ASADA MARINADE

MAKES APPROXIMATELY 2 CUPS / **PREP TIME:** 5 minutes

This is a perfect marinade for tough cuts like skirt steak and flank steak. The acid in the citrus helps break down muscle fibers in the meat for a more tender, flavorful bite.

Juice of 3 large oranges

Juice of 2 limes

Juice of 2 lemons

¼ cup avocado oil

¼ cup apple cider vinegar

¼ cup water

2 tablespoons soy sauce

4 or 5 garlic
   cloves, chopped

1 jalapeño, diced

½ white onion, sliced

½ bunch
   cilantro, chopped

Combine all the ingredients in a large resealable plastic bag or glass bowl and mix thoroughly. Use as directed in your recipe.

USE WITH: Skirt Steak Carne Asada Tacos with Avocado Crema (page 54), Marinated Pulled Quail Tostada (page 124)

POULTRY AND SEAFOOD HERB BRINE

MAKES APPROXIMATELY 1 GALLON / PREP TIME: 10 minutes / **COOK TIME:** 2 minutes

This brine can be used for various meats from chicken, turkey, and Cornish game hens to all types of fish and seafood. Make sure to dissolve all the salt and sugar and to chill it before use.

1 gallon water

1 cup salt

1 cup sugar

5 or 6 garlic cloves, peeled and smashed

3 or 4 rosemary sprigs

3 or 4 sage stems with leaves

1 bunch fresh thyme

Juice of 2 lemons

Combine all the ingredients in a large pot and bring to a boil over high heat. You want the salt and sugar to completely dissolve in the water, about 2 minutes. When the brine comes to a boil and the salt and sugar are dissolved, remove it from the heat and chill.

USE WITH: Smoked Rainbow Trout Dip (page 25), Herb Butter Smoked Turkey Breast (page 106), Whole Smoked Cornish Game Hens (page 108), Brined Turkey BLT Sandwich (page 116), Spatchcocked BBQ Chicken (page 120)

SMOKED GARLIC AIOLI

MAKES APPROXIMATELY 1½ CUPS / **PREP TIME:** 5 minutes / **COOK TIME:** 30 minutes

I love making this aioli on Sunday and having it for the rest of the week to use in recipes and on sandwiches. It's also the perfect dip for chicken wings, seafood, and bacon-wrapped potatoes.

1 head garlic

3 tablespoons olive
   oil, divided

Salt

Freshly ground
   black pepper

1 cup mayonnaise

Juice of 1 lemon

1 tablespoon
   Dijon mustard

USE WITH: Bacon and Brie Stuffed Pork Burger (page 98), Creamy Jalapeño Turkey Burger (page 110), Bacon Wrapped Chicken Wings (page 111), Garlic Butter Lobster Tail Skewers (page 140), Crusted Catfish Po' Boy with Smoked Garlic Aioli (page 152), Bacon-Wrapped Grilled Yukon Potato Wedges (page 168)

1. Set up your grill for indirect cooking (see page 4). Fill a charcoal chimney with lump charcoal and light it with a fire starter cube. When the coals have turned gray, dump them into the grill on the side opposite the disposable aluminum pan, replace the cooking grate, close the lid, and open the top and bottom vents to fully open until the grill temperature registers about 275°F. Continue to monitor the grill, adjusting the vents as needed, until it reaches a cooking temperature of around 300°F.

2. Cut the top off the head of garlic, coat the garlic bulb with 1 tablespoon of olive oil, and season with salt and pepper. Place on the indirect side of the grill and cook the garlic 20 to 30 minutes, until the cloves soften. Insert the end of an instant-read thermometer into one of the garlic cloves; it should be soft and probe easily. Remove from the grill to cool a bit.

3. While the garlic is grilling, combine the mayonnaise, the remaining 2 tablespoons of olive oil, the lemon juice, and Dijon mustard in a bowl and stir until thoroughly blended. Refrigerate until ready to use.

4. Squeeze the softened garlic cloves onto a cutting board. Dice, then smash them with the back of your knife to create a paste. Add the garlic paste to the refrigerated mayonnaise mixture, stirring to combine thoroughly. Taste and add salt and pepper if needed.

MEASUREMENT CONVERSIONS

VOLUME EQUIVALENTS	U.S. STANDARD	U.S. STANDARD (OUNCES)	METRIC (APPROXIMATE)
LIQUID	2 tablespoons	1 fl. oz.	30 mL
	¼ cup	2 fl. oz.	60 mL
	½ cup	4 fl. oz.	120 mL
	1 cup	8 fl. oz.	240 mL
	1½ cups	12 fl. oz.	355 mL
	2 cups or 1 pint	16 fl. oz.	475 mL
	4 cups or 1 quart	32 fl. oz.	1 L
	1 gallon	128 fl. oz.	4 L
DRY	⅛ teaspoon	–	0.5 mL
	¼ teaspoon	–	1 mL
	½ teaspoon	–	2 mL
	¾ teaspoon	–	4 mL
	1 teaspoon	–	5 mL
	1 tablespoon	–	15 mL
	¼ cup	–	59 mL
	⅓ cup	–	79 mL
	½ cup	–	118 mL
	⅔ cup	–	156 mL
	¾ cup	–	177 mL
	1 cup	–	235 mL
	2 cups or 1 pint	–	475 mL
	3 cups	–	700 mL
	4 cups or 1 quart	–	1 L
	½ gallon	–	2 L
	1 gallon	–	4 L

OVEN TEMPERATURES

FAHRENHEIT	CELSIUS (APPROXIMATE)
250°	120°
300°	150°
325°	165°
350°	180°
375°	190°
400°	200°
425°	220°
450°	230°

WEIGHT EQUIVALENTS

U.S. STANDARD	METRIC (APPROXIMATE)
½ ounce	15 g
1 ounce	30 g
2 ounces	60 g
4 ounces	115 g
8 ounces	225 g
12 ounces	340 g
16 ounces or 1 pound	455 g

INDEX

INDEX

INDEX

ACKNOWLEDGMENTS

I would like to thank my family foremost for all your love and support. Thank you to Jason Baker from Green Mountain Grills for believing in me and making me feel like family. Thank you to so many of my barbecue family and friends who have shared with me not only your recipes but also your love of cooking, your homes, and your family. Thank you to everyone who has attended one of my barbecue classes, whether in person or online, and who continues to support my barbecue products. And thank you for buying my book. Thank you all—because of you I can continue to share my knowledge and love of barbecue across the world.

ABOUT THE AUTHOR

 **STERLING SMITH**, US Navy veteran and owner/pitmaster of Loot N' Booty BBQ, has been competing on the professional barbecue circuit since 2009. In that time, Sterling and his family have traveled nationally and internationally to compete in major competitions, including the Jack Daniel's World Championship Invitational BBQ, where he won the title of World Pork Champion; the American Royal World Series of BBQ, where he won Reserve Grand Champion out of more than 450 professional barbecue teams as well as the title of Chicken World Champion; the Sam's Club Finals; and the Australian Brewery Kingsford Invitational. Sterling has won 35 Grand and Reserve Grand Championship awards, more than 400 top 10 awards, 10 perfect "180" scores, and four 700+ scores, and he is the two-time Australian Invitational Lamb Champion. Loot N' Booty BBQ is the 2014, 2015, 2016, and 2017 Arizona BBQ Team of the Year and was featured on an episode of the Discovery Channel/Destination America's series *Smoked*, where Sterling and his wife, Molly, won the title of "Smoked BBQ Boss." Loot N' Booty BBQ rubs and sauces are sold at hundreds of retailers worldwide, and Sterling teaches competition and backyard-style barbecue classes at locations across the world. For more information, visit LootNBootyBBQ.com.

CPSIA information can be obtained
at www.ICGtesting.com
Printed in the USA
JSHW012334081021
19413JS00002B/3